Best Practices for Teaching with Emerging Technologies

As social media and Web 2.0 technologies continue to transform the learning trends and preferences of students, educators need to understand the applicability of these new tools in all types of learning environments. *Best Practices for Teaching with Emerging Technologies* will provide both new and experienced online, hybrid, and face-to-face instructors with:

- Practical examples of how low-cost and free technologies can be used to support student learning
- Best practices for integrating web-based tools into a course management system and managing student privacy in a Web 2.0 environment
- "Showcase" spotlights woven throughout the book, providing examples of how the tools described in the book are already being used effectively in educational settings
- An easy-to-reference format, organized with visual icons used to delineate each tool's visual, video, voice, and mobile features
- Ideas for integrating mobile learning into your students' learning experiences

This practical, easy-to-use guide will serve the needs of both two- and four-year college educators seeking to refresh or transform their instruction. Readers will be rewarded with an ample yet manageable collection of proven emerging technologies that can be leveraged for generating content, enhancing communications with and between students, and cultivating participatory, student-centered learning activities.

Michelle Pacansky-Brock received the 2007 Sloan-C Excellence in Online Teaching Award, a 2007 NISOD award for Teaching Excellence, a Sloan-C Effective Practice Award in 2010 for her use of VoiceThread, and the Capella Educator Advancement scholarship in 2011. Her current projects and interests include teaching the history of photography online, facilitating online faculty development courses, consulting for companies and colleges, supporting statewide faculty training and educational technology integration efforts in California, and completing an EdD in Educational Leadership and Management. Learn more about Michelle at http://www.teaching withoutwalls.com

Best Practices in Online Teaching and Learning Series
Susan Ko, Series Editor

Online education continues to rapidly expand as a diverse group of higher education institutions and non-profit and governmental entities adopt both fully online and blended learning. As a result there has likewise been tremendous growth in the need for special preparation and training for instructors in the methods and approaches to teaching online–moving beyond the emphasis on software training that once comprised a large portion of training for online teachers. Many instructors seek introductory, yet comprehensive professional development books that coincide with the next stages in their online teaching careers. While they are interested in principles and tips that are grounded in evidence-based research, they do not necessarily want to wade through research in order to formulate the applications that constitute best practices.

Enter Routledge's *Best Practices in Online Teaching and Learning* series, which provides in-depth coverage of focused areas and issues educators might confront in the ever-changing environment of online teaching and learning. Based on the solid experience of expert practitioners and communicated in a jargon-free, popular style, titles in this series will address the most current issues and trends in online teaching and learning. Each title is designed to be rich in examples drawn from experienced, real-life online instructors, exemplifying a best practices approach and lending themselves to easy application by the reader.

The Best Practices concept provides a unifying element in the series and offers more in-depth coverage than existing book series on similar topics. By covering both depth and breadth of content, books in the series will be introductory enough to be of interest to those relatively new to online education yet rigorous enough to appeal to those seeking further professional development and knowledge in this area.

Titles:
Michelle Pacansky-Brock · *Best Practices for Teaching with Emerging Technologies*

Forthcoming Titles:
Husein Abdul-Hamid & Ouanessa Boubsil · *Best Instructional Practices for Teaching Online*

Best Practices for Teaching with Emerging Technologies

Michelle Pacansky-Brock

Edited by Susan Ko

Routledge
Taylor & Francis Group

NEW YORK AND LONDON

First published 2013
by Routledge
711 Third Avenue, New York, NY 10017

Simultaneously published in the UK
by Routledge
2 Park Square, Milton Park, Abingdon, Oxon OX14 4RN

Routledge is an imprint of the Taylor & Francis Group, an informa business

Library of Congress Cataloging in Publication Data
Pacansky-Brock, Michelle.
  Best practices for teaching with emerging technologies /
  Michelle Pacansky-Brock ; edited by Susan Ko.
      p. cm. – (Best practices in online teaching and learning)
  Includes bibliographical references and index.
  1. Educational technology. I. Ko, Susan Schor. II. Title.
  LB1028.3.P22 2012
  371.33–dc23   2012010915

ISBN: 978–0–415–89938–3 (hbk)
ISBN: 978–0–415–89939–0 (pbk)
ISBN: 978–0–203–09596–6 (ebk)

Typeset in Bembo and Gill Sans
by Swales & Willis Ltd, Exeter, Devon

This book is dedicated to my past students
for making me the teacher I am and to my future
students for making me the teacher I will become.

Contents

Preface

Writing a print-based book about emerging technologies may seem like a bit of a contradiction to you. And in some ways, you are right depending on how you define "emerging." For our task here, "emerging technologies" are tools or types of tools that are making an impact in teaching and learning but are not yet adopted in mainstream teaching practices. In essence, the technologies focused on here will fall into one or more of the categories of cloud-based, Web 2.0, social media, and mobile apps. Cloud-based refers to applications that are stored and accessed through the web and provide the flexibility to be accessed from anywhere with an internet connection. Web 2.0 means web-based tools that are easy to use and create with, and possess collaborative and social sharing capabilities. Social media refers to web-based or mobile technologies that turn communication into a participatory experience. Finally, mobile apps are those applications that are designed to be used on a mobile device like a smartphone or tablet.

Some of these tools are likely already familiar to you—like Twitter and YouTube-while others may be introduced to you for the first time by this book.

The popularization of emerging technology tools have dramatically affected the way people around the world communicate and share. They also make the creation of multimedia content simple and straightforward; transforming each of us into a multimedia content creator and facilitating connecting and sharing with others, whether in the classroom or the global community, in an instant.

And mobile apps hold exciting opportunities for new teaching and learning methods, including support for learners with cognitive and physical disabilities. While many professors and administrators assume smartphones are only tools for affluent student populations, studies reveal that lower socio-economic groups are among the most likely to purchase a smartphone, as it offers cost-saving access to a bundle of media services including voice, sms (texting), and internet.[1]

Every week new technology tools are released to the public and users of all kinds, including educational technology enthusiasts, begin to experiment with them. The tools that offer potential in teaching and learning begin to pick up popularity through the educational blogosphere and "Twitterverse." Over time, some educators begin to experiment with them in their classes. Then, in typical start up fashion, many of them disappear, some of the good ones are acquired by other companies, and others continue to play a role in learning. The latter category is the focus of this book. It wouldn't be prudent to explore bleeding-edge technologies in a print format, due to the delay in the book writing and publication process, and it wouldn't be an effective topic to share with you, when our focus is on "best practices."

If you're looking for some reassurance about whether or not these tools will stick around for the long haul, unfortunately, there is no way to predict the life expectancy of any tool showcased in this book and that is not my intended goal. Further, this book is not intended to serve primarily as a guide to emerging tools. As a college instructor who has used emerging technologies in her classes for years, one thing is crystal clear to me-*using* tools well is not the same as *teaching* well with emerging tools. This book focuses on *teaching* effectively with emerging technologies. It places an important emphasis on the student experience, provides a framework for evaluating tools, and shares stories, tips, and showcase samples from my own and other instructors' classes.

This book is written for college educators who are teaching or will be teaching online, face-to-face, and/or hybrid classes—the complex reality of most 21st-century educators! The ideas and strategies shared here are intended to spark curiosity inside you and inspire you to see the array of learning possibilities emerging technologies hold for the future of college learning. This is an amazing time to be teaching—we are at a juncture between centuries-old traditions and fresh, untouched territory. At once, our classrooms are both relics of antiquated traditions and symbols of the future of a global society. The popularization of online and hybrid classes can mean recycling our traditions and translating them into digital formats or it can mean embracing the profession of teaching as a "practice" in which we value experimentation and innovation and discover the unexpected which may completely redefine our concept of "a good class." The choice is yours. This book is written to inspire the latter.

To get us started, the introduction of this book takes you on an inspirational journey through my own teaching transformation. I reflect openly and honestly about why I elected to integrate Web 2.0 tools into my courses when they were becoming popular in 2007. Also included in the introduction is an overview of my 2009 "flipped classroom" teaching experiment in which I shifted *all* of my lectures online, encouraged students to use their iPod, iPhone, or computer to access them, and used class time for discussion, analysis, and debate. You'll have the chance to reflect on my students' feedback and explore some surprising discoveries I uncovered in the findings.

In Chapter 1, we lay the groundwork for teaching with emerging technologies and examine strategies and techniques for ensuring your students get started on a successful foot. Some of this involves rethinking your class philosophy and writing new, community-oriented ground rules that both you and your students will model throughout the class. Also included in this chapter are some important fundamentals about student privacy, embedding content (vs. linking to it) and teaching with copyrighted material—essential topics you'll want to get your arms around early.

In Chapter 2, we examine the possibilities embedded in effective uses of emerging technologies to reinvent college learning. Using Barr and Tagg's 1995 *From Teaching to Learning* as a framework, the chapter explores how collaborative, mobile Web 2.0 tools and social media technologies have affected the way social change occurs, the way we socialize, and the way we learn. Chapter 2 also reviews some of the essential criteria to consider when evaluating tools to use in your classes in support of your goals.

Chapters 3, 4 and 5 provide an introduction to an array of tools. Chapter 3 illuminates a selection of essential tools that are recommended for all professors, regardless of your discipline or goals. In Chapters 4 and 5, you will find a rich collection of tools organized around a common theme. The tools in Chapter 4 are resources for you to teach beyond text-opening your online communications and activities into the realm of voice and video and increasing your students' engagement and your own social presence in the process. Chapter 5 takes the conversation one step further by presenting an overview of tools that facilitate your transition into creating a truly student-centered, participatory learning experience. Within Chapters 4 and 5, you will find plenty of learning "showcases" that demonstrate specific ways that professors are using the tools highlighted in the book-providing practical examples for your own teaching.

Chapter 6 zooms back out again and traces the pulse and future of mobile learning in college. Mobile learning is making an extraordinary splash across the world. According to the Pre Research center, 46% of adults in the United States owned a smartphone in 2012. And it's reshaping the workforce and, in turn, the skills our students will need to be successful in their future careers. Chapter 6 will intrigue you to see a smartphone as something other than a nuisance in your classroom and pique your curiosity about how tablet PCs can be used to foster more collaborative college classroom experiences for students. Finally, Chapter 6 includes a provocative and important reflection about how mobile apps and tablet PCs are being used by people with learning and physical disabilities to empower them to live more independently and *learn* in a way that supports their unique needs. Are mobile devices the pathway to a truly inclusive model of college learning that meets the needs of all learners?

Finally, Chapter 7 is a concise reference to ensure you know how to locate the robust collection of web-based resources that support this book. The resources are not printed because they will remain a living, evolving collection and will continue to grow and shift just as quickly as 21st-century teaching does!

Acknowledgments

I would like to acknowledge the support and guidance of Susan Ko, series editor, for seeing something in me and extending the opportunity to author this book. Susan's advice, feedback, and contributions to the field of online teaching and learning have guided and motivated me throughout this journey. I would also like to thank Alex Masulis of Routledge for his assistance and timely responses to my frequent questions. And I am grateful for the generosity of Rose Basubas, a former student and rising star, for designing the book's cover.

A thank you is also due to my husband, Stan, for his unwavering support and encouragement; to my parents, Jake and Nancy, for instilling the drive in me to follow my heart; and to my boys, two digital natives, whose questions and observations teach me to continue to see the world in new ways and who serve as my inspiration for standing up for what I believe in.

Finally, I extend a warm thank you to all the faculty who were willing to share their teaching experiments with me and contribute to this book. Your commitment to improving your students' learning, your dedication to openness through the sharing of your ideas in blog posts, Tweets, articles, conference presentations, and responses to my individual inquiries have made this book a valuable resource to many.

Michelle Pacansky-Brock

Introduction

The Flipped Classroom

"Students today are unmotivated."

"Students today don't care about anything but their grades."

"Students today feel entitled and aren't willing to work hard."

Have you found yourself saying or thinking any of these things? If so, you are experiencing the effects of significant problems in higher education. This chapter will attempt to unpack statements like these by examining them within a social context and reframing them as symptoms of pervasive problems in higher education, rather than an entire generation of lost souls. We will examine learning within the fabric of a society that has been transformed from the inside out by emerging technologies and ask whether or not our current learning practices are still relevant in light of these sweeping changes. To put that another way, are our students the problem? Or is it our instructional model?

This chapter serves as our initial exploration into some of the ways "emerging technologies" are reinvisioning college learning. In the context of this book, emerging technologies are defined as tools that fall into one or more of the following four categories: cloud-based applications, that are easily stored online and accessible from anywhere with an internet connection; Web 2.0 tools, that make the creation and sharing of multimedia content simple; social media, technologies that transform communication into a highly interactive experience; and mobile apps, applications that are designed to operate on mobile devices (smartphones or tablets). The tools featured in this book have demonstrated potential to enhance college learning by making it easier for instructors and students to create and share multimedia content and make learning more interactive and collaborative.

As educators, it's common for us to teach the way *we* were taught and it can be challenging to step outside of our practice to reflect on and analyze our teaching approaches. But doing so can be an enlightening experience. This book will take you for a ride through my own journey of enlightenment that inspired me to see my teaching practices from a new perspective.

There are particular catalysts I encountered throughout my journey that jarred me just enough to pause and consider whether or not I was doing the very best I could to meet the diverse needs of my students. One of those catalysts was an article written by Barr and Tagg in 1995, which I reflect on more deeply in Chapter 2. In their article,

"From Teaching to Learning," the authors examine how our underlying assumptions and traditions inform the very outcomes of our practice. And they argue that a paradigm shift, from teaching to learning, is occurring across education. As we consider this argument roughly two decades later, I think it's safe to say that the paradigm has not changed dramatically—but I do believe that the transformations brought about through digital, mobile technologies outside the walls of our classrooms are accelerating the urgency for this paradigm shift.

Paradigm shifts can be painfully difficult, as they require a complete overhaul to the foundations that inform our processes and traditions. According to Barr and Tagg, they are most likely to occur when two indicators are present:

1. When "difficulties or anomalies begin to appear in the functioning of the existing paradigm which cannot be handled adequately."
2. When an alternative paradigm surfaces "that will account for all that the original paradigm accounts for . . . and [that] offers real hope for solving the major difficulties facing the current paradigm."[1]

I argue that low student engagement and motivation is a difficulty that college professors face as a result of using class time to deliver passive lecture content to our students who are thirsty for something different. And the desire to ward off student use of mobile devices in the classroom is another difficulty that continues to create friction within the functioning of our current paradigm. Here we will unpack these difficulties by examining the way accelerated technological changes have resulted in deep-rooted shifts in generational preferences that exacerbate the way students and professors relate to college classes. We will also consider the lecture within the context of brain research and explore the ways that emerging technologies can be used to foster the type of multisensory learning that *all* of our brains crave.

Additionally, by sharing a case study from my own college teaching, I offer an alternative paradigm, the "flipped classroom," a term that was first used by two high school chemistry teachers, Jonathan Bergmann and Aaron Sams, around 2007, and has become increasingly popular through the work of Salman Khan and the Khan Academy, which provides open access to thousands of instructional videos about topics from math to art history.[2] The flipped classroom model uses video recordings of lectures that are shared with students *before* class time, freeing up face-to-face time to interact with students and apply the information learned in the videos. Ultimately, classroom time is transformed from a passive to an active experience and the role of the instructor shifts from "sage on the stage" to "guide on the side." This chapter provides insight, guidance and an essential toolkit for instructors who wish to get started with transforming their learning model.

This chapter is intended to open your eyes to the possibilities emerging technologies hold for changing the way college has been taught for hundreds of years and to possible ways that instructors might transform their own teaching.

Tectonic Generational Shifts

I am a member of Generation X. I was born in 1971—the year the microprocessor was invented, Greenpeace was formed, Ms. Magazine originated, the voting age in the US was lowered from 21 to 18, Walt Disney World opened, the FDA approved soft contact lenses, and the US Supreme Court upheld a controversial measure to bus children in an effort to desegregate minority populations. Like you, the events and experiences of my generation played an important role in shaping who I am today.

Growing up in the heart of California's Silicon Valley, technology has always played a major role in my life. I have many vivid memories that mark some of the ways technology has influenced me. My dad had a long career as a research scientist at IBM. His home office was just below my bedroom and late at night, I would often hear a high-pitched squelch when he would dial in on his modem and connect to the "mainframe" computer. At the time, that noise was simply annoying to me but now I can appreciate what he was doing. In the early 1980s, my dad was among the small group of American employees who continued to work from home after leaving the office. In those pre-PC days, having a computer at home was rare and having one that was connected to a network was an anomaly.

I also remember one evening when my dad called me into his office and pointed my eyes towards the large computer on his desk. He leaned towards me and pointed at a few bright green words that were moving horizontally across the black screen and said, "That's a message from my co-worker." I didn't understand the complexity of that statement but I can remember how completely stunned and exhilarated I was as I stared at those words. "You mean, you're talking to someone on that screen who isn't here?" I asked. The prospect of communicating with another person at a distance through a computer dazzled me.

I also remember the excitement I felt in grade school when my parents rented our first VCR from the neighborhood video store. VCRs were *expensive* and renting one for brief periods was the only way we could have the luxury of watching a movie we selected from the shelves of the video store. We lugged it home in a big black carrying case, figured out how to operate it, and huddled together on our family room sofa as we anticipated watching a movie that we selected together. And while early VCRs did have the ability to rewind and fast-forward, doing so required one to get up off the couch and manually turn the dial. And when the phone rang during the movie, our choices were to get up and answer it because it was attached to a wall (and we had no idea, by the way, who was on the other end) or just let it ring—voicemail and answering machines weren't in the picture yet.

I compare that to the context in which my own children are growing up and the contrast is staggering. Before my husband and I made the move to DVR, my boys complained that our TV was "broken" because they couldn't rewind the shows as they watched them. Now that we have DVR, all of us have newfound expectations about watching television. We purposely avoid sitting down and watching a show at its airing time because watching advertisements is, well, a waste of time. Rather, we record specific shows and watch them at a time that fits into our schedule, which also extends the convenience of fast forwarding through all the commercials to watch a 60-minute show in 45 minutes.

Additionally, the emergence of iPods around 2005 not only shifted the paradigm of the music industry, putting corporations (like Tower Records, an icon of my generation) who didn't change along with the times out of business, but also dramatically altered a user's listening experience. I was in fifth grade when MTV launched. I remember sitting in front of the TV for hours waiting to see my favorite videos be played. My experiences were controlled by the decisions of the VJ (arguably, choices are still controlled today by media corporations but this fact is much more transparent than it used to be). And when my favorite videos were played, I would click "record" on my 25-pound boom box and capture the song's audio on my tape cassette. (Yes, I now realize that was copyright infringement but I don't recall a critical discourse about this problem when I was a child.) Those cassettes were treasures to me. I took pride in the personalized music collection I had created and would scribble a customized title like "Michelle's Mix—1, 2, etc." on the front of each tape—and even make copies of the tapes for my best friends. There is no doubt in my mind that I was thirsty for personalized experiences, much like today's youth are.

In contrast, there has been copious literature written about the Millennial generation, people born between 1980–2000. Millennials comprise the traditional college age student population (18–24) but, each year, their age creeps further and further into the age group that is considered "non-traditional." For example, in 2012, the oldest Millennials are 32 years old. And as 21st-century professors, you have the daunting task of teaching the *most generationally diverse group of college students ever.*

Keeping in mind the ways that one's use of technology informs her preferences and expectations, here are a few statistics to paint a portrait of how Millennials are using technology. Ninety-four percent of Millennials are internet users (compared to 78% of all Americans over age 18) and out of these, 74% have broadband at home (compared to 61% overall), 94% have a cell phone (compared to 83% overall), 63% own a game console (compared to 42% overall), and 70% have a laptop (compared to 56% overall). In 2011, 51% of Millennials had a smartphone, compared to 35% of the overall adult population. Eighty-one percent have wireless access to the internet (compared to 59% overall), 83% are active users of social networking (compared to 65% overall) and they outperform other generations in all of the following social networking activities: logging in every day, "liking" content multiple times a day, tagging and commenting on photos every day, commenting on other users' statuses every day, and curating a network comprised of users of a diverse socio-economic composition.[3]

Interestingly, despite the common perception that the internet is ruining society (creating a generation of disrespectful, entitled, copyright pirates), adult internet users in the United States are more likely than non-internet users to be active in a volunteer group or organization (86% compared to 56%). [4] Millennials have become adults while forming social interactions in both the physical and online realms. Going online is not task-driven for them; rather, it's an experience that welcomes them to find communities of users who share their interests. "Online" is a culture to the Millennial generation. Yet to most colleges, it is a delivery method.

The rich options and highly personalized, community-oriented experiences of Millennials have informed their expectations and preferences. Millennials prefer to understand why they are engaging in an activity and seek out clear expectations in advance. I am familiar with the tension these characteristics can cause in college classrooms that are founded upon a top-down hierarchical model in which the professor dictates what students will do and the students are expected to be quiet and do it. This is one of the reasons Chapter 1 of this book included tips for cultivating a community-oriented classroom.

Let's take this one step further and take a peek at the generation following the Millennials. My two children are both members of the post-Millennial generation—a generation that is yet to be named (but one early suggestion is the "Homelanders").[5] They are the first generation to be raised within a truly digital society and while we cannot identify their unifying characteristics yet, the Center for Generational Studies predicts that they will likely be the most "racially and culturally diverse generation in US history" and because of "advances in global communication, they may be the most transient generation as well." While it may feel difficult to begin to plan for their arrival when we're still panting to keep up with the Millennial generation, now is the time.

My "post-Millennial" children, born in 2000 and 2002, received their own iPod between the age of seven and eight. That iPod can hold thousands of songs, all selected by the owner. The songs can be added as audio-only or a user can select to purchase and upload the song's video instead. The iPod also holds TV shows, full-length movies, audio books, and digital pictures—and includes a video camera! All that and it's smaller than the comb I used to carry in my back pocket in middle school. The iPod is only a tool—a piece of technology. But it has re-sculpted the meaning of "personalization" to this generation (I didn't mention that each of my boys has an iPod in their favorite color too). Ask yourself this: if your earliest music experiences involved the option to curate your very own audio and video collection and you had access to it at any time and in any place, would you be as motivated to sit by the radio and listen to songs *someone else* has decided to play for you? That's very similar to the motivation and engagement problem we have in college today. It's not that students aren't willing to work hard—I just don't believe that. I've seen amazing passion, dynamism, and effort in my students' work and I've seen glazed, detached stares—the difference resides in the type of learning environment I use to engage them.

Julie Evans is the director of Project Tomorrow, a non-profit organization that facilitates the annual *Speak Up* survey which tracks and analyzes trends in K-12 student learning by surveying nearly 300,000 students each year. Since 2005 the survey has had its finger on the pulse of student use of technology and its correlation with learning preferences. In 2005, according to the survey, half of the sixth graders who were surveyed owned a cell phone. In 2010, that statistic held true but an additional one third of them owned a smartphone. Even more stunning is the fact that nearly a quarter of students in kindergarten through second grade had a cell phone and 16% had a smart phone. Twenty-five percent of sixth graders used an e-textbook, while half took tests online, three times as many had taken an online class in 2010 compared to those who did in 2005, and nearly half of 6th-grade girls and over a third of boys regularly updated their social networking site (a 125% increase since 2005) even though they aren't legally old enough to use one.[6]

K-12 educators are exploring the possibilities of these shifts, particularly students' interest in "untethered learning," defined as learning that occurs from anywhere at anytime and it's directly correlated with the widespread use of mobile devices that began around 2005 with the popularity of iPods. Mobile learning in higher education is discussed more explicitly in Chapter 6.

The Engagement Problem

Back in 2006, a student of mine approached me after class one day and asked if I had heard of a website called YouTube. When I said no, she went on to explain to me that it's a website that allows people to upload videos and share them with each other. I can remember thinking, "So? Why on earth would people want to watch other people's videos? How is that revolutionary?"

At the time of this writing, YouTube reports that over 3 billion videos are viewed on YouTube a day by users 18–54 years old in 25 different countries and 43 languages. More video is uploaded to YouTube in one month than the three major US networks made in 60 years.[7] I guess it's safe to say I was wrong.

Outside the walls of the classroom, most college students learn through flat, interconnected, and highly personalized experiences. Millennials are accustomed to learning from their peers in a virtual community in which their opinions and ideas matter. This model dramatically contradicts the traditional, hierarchic, top-down model imposed in most college classrooms. If technology can deliver the same message in a better, more personalized, convenient way—that meets not only the preferences of a student, but also his/her individualized learning needs—then why are we not exploring or at least contemplating this as an opportunity to transform teaching and learning?

Howard Rheingold, professor at Stanford and Berkeley, author of several books including *Smartmobs*, and the creator of the *Social Media Classroom*, has influenced my thinking about the significance of teaching with social media. I had the opportunity to meet Rheingold at a conference in 2010 but he influenced me long before that through the videos he openly shares on YouTube. I have enjoyed listening to his presentations on my iPhone during my routine walks through my neighborhood. Early on, his messages about the importance of cultivating a "crap detector" in our students resonated with me. To summarize Rheingold, a "crap detector" is the ability to discern valid digital content from meaningless, well, crap. He's right—and, yet, where are our students learning this skill?

The other Rheingold message that has stuck with me most is his willingness to be blunt about the purpose of a face-to-face college class. Rheingold says, "I ask [my students] on the first day of class, why are we standing here? Why do we all come to this physical place? Do you rush home at 7:00 at night to watch your favorite TV show or do you record it?" Rheingold is reshaping his teaching paradigm to align with the expectations of his students but also to make the time he spends with them more effective and productive. He continues, "[I]f I have an hour's worth of lecture, as teachers have had for the past thousand years, I'll put it on YouTube which has not existed for a thousand years."[8] By recording his lecture content (with a simple webcam and a free YouTube account) and sharing it with his students prior to class, he "flips" his classroom from a passive to an active experience. Rheingold is, by no means, the first or only educator to use the flipped classroom model—he's one of the many experimenting with the concept. In a flipped classroom, coming to class on Tuesday and Thursday for an hour and a half becomes an active experience that is grounded in discussion, debate, and analysis, rather than 90 minutes of passive listening.

If you have felt like your students do the minimal work they can just to get by and get a good (or decent) grade, you're right. But this is partly because we have constructed a model that enables them to do so. Imagine a different paradigm—one like Rheingold's that uses emerging technologies to have students watch your lectures online (from a laptop, phone or tablet) and complete a formative assessment before coming to class. One in which you could review the results of the formative assessment and then make a list of proficiencies that have not been mastered and use class time to work through them actively with your students. *Why do we not do this?*

Michael Wesch, an anthropology professor at Kansas State University who was named 2008 U.S. Professor of the Year by the Carnegie Foundation for the Advancement of Teaching, is, perhaps, best known for his 2007 video "Visions of Students Today" (which, at the time of writing this, has received 4.5 million views on YouTube). The video pans through a large lecture hall and zooms in on the wall which reveals a hand-written question, "If these walls could talk, what would they say?" Then individual students reveal brief written messages to the camera. One says, "My average class size is 115." Others reveal, "18% of my teachers know my name," "I buy $100 text books that I never open," and, "When I graduate, I will have a job that doesn't exist today." The five-minute video paints a picture of college learning as irrelevant and ineffective at meeting the future goals of 21st-century students.

Both Rheingold and Wesch see the possibilities that emerging technologies hold in reshaping college into an experience that actively engages students in their learning, puts them in the driving seat, and fosters the critical thinking skills necessary for 21st-century success.

Brain-Friendly Learning

 Another benefit of teaching with emerging technologies is the potential they hold for crafting multisensory learning experiences, which are more akin to the way the brain is wired to learn. Teaching to support the way the human brain works? What a concept! John Medina, an affiliate Professor of Bioengineering at the University of Washington School of Medicine and director of the Brain Center for Applied Learning Research at Seattle Pacific University, has extracted the essentials of decades of brain research and compiled what we know about how the brain learns into twelve concise rules. Published in text format as a book titled, *Brain Rules,* and communicated in true multisensory fashion online at http://brainrules.net, Medina's modules serve as a clear, concise guide to illuminate just what's so backwards about formal education. Medina argues that, as a society, we "ignore how the brain works" and the only scandal is "why we're not fixing it." In fact, if you were to envision a large group of students sitting passively in a classroom listening or writing for long periods of time, you would be picturing an "almost perfect anti-brain learning environment," according to Medina.

Here are three of Medina's "brain rules" that are relevant for 21st-century college educators and a few of my own thoughts about how emerging technologies can assist us with developing more brain-friendly learning.

1. Exercise Boosts Brain Power

When we are active, the human brain releases chemicals that increase cognitive functions. When do you get your best ideas? Most likely it's when you're active—at the gym, going for a run, walking to the bus stop, cleaning the floor, making dinner. Incorporating opportunities for students to use mobile devices in their learning experiences—whether you're teaching a face-to-face, online, or hybrid class—extends students the option to learn while participating in their daily activities.

Mobile content has potential to transform passive listening into an experience that can be engaged during physical activity. Imagine if lectures were assigned to students as homework and students could listen to them on a mobile device. Do you think they'd sit in one spot and listen? That certainly would be an option, and one way to make a long commute more productive, but it also opens up the opportunity to listen while out for a jog, walking the dog, cooking dinner, or vacuuming the floor.

2. Sensory Integration[9]

Imagine a picture of a brain. When that brain is exposed to each of the five senses-seeing, hearing, listening, tasting, and smelling—a different region of the brain is activated. The more senses that are engaged in an experience, the more a brain is stimulated and the longer a person remembers what has occurred. Simply, if you were a student in a class listening to a professor, you'd remember less than a student in the next class listening to the same lecture supplemented with images, and even less than a student sitting in a third classroom who was listening to the lecture, viewing images, and stimulated with text. Unisensory learning never beats multisensory learning.

This is compelling for many reasons. All of us (not just traditional college-age students) are now able to learn through video, images and text and many of us can do so using the mobile device in our pocket. The tools to create multisensory learning have never been more accessible to the general public and using them no longer requires one to be a multimedia production expert. If we're serious about learning, this is the brain rule we will take seriously.

3. Vision Trumps All Other Senses[10]

Each of the senses enhances learning but the human brain particularly loves images. Humans are visual creatures. We began creating visual representations of our world tens of thousands of years before we devised written languages. Referencing brain research from the 1960s, Medina lucidly states, "Hear a piece of information, and three days later you'll remember 10% of it. Add a picture and you'll remember 65%." This is the underlying reason why advertisements are visual!

In contrast, when most college professors employ a "visual" teaching aid, they're usually inclined to develop a Powerpoint presentation. Powerpoint certainly has the potential to create a compelling visual experience. However, rather than using Powerpoint to craft a dynamic visual backdrop to a verbal presentation, most of us fill the slides with text.

Medina's advice is to delete your Powerpoints and create new ones. That is one approach but there are many other tools that foster visually centric content creation, capsizing the traditional hierarchy of text to image (see Chapter 4 for tips!).

Our recent shift from a mechanical, industrial to a digital, information society has resulted in extreme shifts in preferences and expectations, a reconceptualization of the most effective use of face-to-face time for teaching, and advances in cloud computing and audio-visual technologies have yielded easy to create, multi-sensory experiences that support the way the human brain is wired. These three elements will continue to shake the foundation of the traditional "instructional" paradigm in which higher education is rooted. We have two roads ahead of us and only one leads to a truly transformed paradigm. Which is your path?

Putting it All Together—a Flipped Classroom Experiment

Between 2006 and 2009, my online classes went through a transformation. An arduous recovery from open-heart surgery in early 2006 left me with much time to spare and reduced physical capacity. While I didn't know it at the time, within the coming months, the internet as I knew it would be revolutionized and transform from a static information repository to an interactive, authoring platform facilitating dialogue and connections between people anywhere in the world. This was the dawn of Web 2.0, one of the most provocative social shifts brought about by technology since the introduction of the printing press.

Before my eyes, blogs began to appear everywhere and podcasts were all the rage. Everyone and anyone now had an open invitation to becoming an author. In that timeframe, I spent a lot of time walking, and rather than listening to music, I began to listen to educational podcasts and archives of conference presentations. Within a very short period, I was amazed at how much I had learned from scholars and thought-leaders who had shared these simple audio files. This was a profound moment for me.

I remembered sitting in my office with one of my students the semester prior, feeling agitated that he was rude enough to keep one iPod bud inserted in an ear while having a conversation with me. Those damn iPods were everywhere and they were "distracting my students," I thought. But now I saw things differently. Now I understood the possibilities hidden in the popularization of iPods. This could be a tool I could use to share content with my students and empower them to learn from anywhere.

So, I learned how to create podcasts and then leveraged each of the written lectures I had composed for my online classes as transcripts and turned each of them into a podcast episode. I originally hosted these on a personal site, as my institution did not provide me with an online hosting option, and linked them into my course management system for students to view online or export onto their iPod for a mobile learning experience. But I didn't get rid of the written lectures; instead, I provided both options to students and let them guide their learning and choose the format that worked best for their unique needs.

The second significant change I made was the integration of VoiceThread, a tool that enables online conversations in voice, video, or text around media, into my online classes. As an online art history professor, I was challenged to meet my pedagogical goals within the text-dominant course management system I was using. I could sense that the text-dominated discussion forums were not effective in achieving my course's learning objectives. I needed an environment that could connect students with images and allowed them to visually analyze a painting while commenting on it—something that just doesn't happen fluidly in a discussion forum. When I saw the VoiceThread interface, I knew I had found what I was seeking. VoiceThread creates a conversation space centered around slides that each contain a piece of media (an image, presentation slide, video, document, etc.). The conversations are asynchronous (time-shifted), allowing users to collaborate at a time that is convenient for them, and comments may be left in text, voice (with a microphone or a telephone), or in video with a webcam.

I am often asked, "How do you find out about all these different tools?" Well, through my participation in social media. In 2006, I learned about VoiceThread from a blog post written by Beth Harris, who is now employed as a dean at the Khan Academy after spearheading the creation of Smarthistory, a compelling open educational alternative to a traditional art history textbook, with her colleague Steve Zucker. I commented on Beth's blog, thanking her for sharing VoiceThread with me. Within a very short time, Beth wrote back and asked me if I'd like to collaborate on a VoiceThread.

Within a day, she created a new VoiceThread that included several different views of a 15th-century Flemish painting, *The Arnolfini Portrait*, by Jan van Eyck. Beth left the first comment and then emailed me letting me know it was my turn. Later that day, I clicked on the link to the VoiceThread, logged into my account, listened to her comment, and left a voice comment in response to hers. We continued our back and forth dialogue for the first couple of days, at times that were convenient for both of us (she is in New York and I'm in California). Then Beth invited two colleagues of hers to join us, art historians from the east coast. We continued with a discussion about the painting, applying our own perspectives and a variety of art historical methodologies. The collaboration was not only fun and inspiring for me, it actually produced a collaborative learning resource that I shared with my students in future semesters. This product allowed for my students to listen into a conversation between a group of art historians about a painting—so much richer than having me lecture to them about it! You can view the collaboration here if you're interested: http://voicethread.com/share/3511/.

Participating in that collaborative VoiceThread with Beth and her colleagues was pivotal for me. It put me in the seat of both a *teacher* and a *learner*. It opened the blinds and showed me how easily I could collaborate with others, at a distance, in voice and video (and for free). It gave me confidence and helped me understand that even though I was an art historian, not an audio/video web specialist, I could find tools that enabled me to convey my social presence to my online students and offer new, exciting pedagogical models.

I reflected deeply on the provocative shifts in learning that were occurring in my life as a result of emerging technologies and, little by little, began to reconstruct my online classes. Why my *online* classes and not my *face-to-face* classes? That's a great question. Probably the best answer is simply because it felt most natural to me to embrace web-technologies in my web-based classes. By mid-2007, I had transformed my online classes by integrating podcasts, VoiceThreads, and pulling students into a media-rich blogging experience in Ning. (Ning provides a method for anyone to create a private social network. At the time it was free but now it's a premium tool.) I felt like a chef who had been granted a new spice rack filled with magical seasonings. My students' feedback exhilarated me and the high level of student participation was enough to make me pause and realize *there is a better way of doing things*. Ironically, I was surrounded by a deeply concerned institutional discussion about low online success and retention rates while mine had steadily increased to over 80%.

That year, I was honored with the Sloan-C Excellence in Online Teaching Award which was an important moment for me. Like many (most?) professors, I was teaching in solitude, making changes and revisions to my courses within a vacuum. As much as I wanted to peek at what others were doing so I could learn from them and share my own work, I didn't have a context to do so. I was excited about my online classes and was thirsty to be part of a community focused on exploring the meaning of "quality online teaching"—rather than dwelling on what's wrong with online classes.

Receiving the Sloan-C Award empowered me because I was able to have my courses be evaluated within the context of a national conversation about quality online learning and, as a result, I felt more confident and began to share what I was doing with other educators. In 2007, I began my own blog and started to share my ideas and my students' feedback with the global educational community. That would be my path to finding the community I had been seeking. Sharing became my fuel for my own lifelong learning—a way for me to give back to a community from which I had learned so much. And the more I contributed, the more I gained through the connections I made.

While the engagement and learning in my *online* classes soared to new heights, my *face-to-face* classes had changed very little. They were still, for the most part, comprised of lectures with some online assignments (view this move, review this website, etc.). I felt an increasing tension each time I delivered a lecture in person that I had already developed as a mobile podcast episode. "Why am I doing this?" I would ask myself.

For a long time, I struggled to figure out how to make sense of this problem. My internal dialogue went something like this, "I'm lecturing to my students. I'm spending my time with them to deliver the same information I have recorded as audio podcasts. This feels redundant. But if I give them access to the mobile lectures, they won't come to class. Why should they? But why should I lecture to them when this information is available in a method that will likely help them learn more effectively by extending the option to pause, replay and rewind?" I was stuck and didn't know what to do.

I also felt frustrated with my students' passivity. Online, my students were participatory and interactive. Offline, most of them would enter class, recline in their seats, and stare at me with glazed eyes. I'd spend my time with them fighting to keep them engaged—breaking up long lectures with video clips, small and large group discussions, using writing prompts—and these things helped but they were by no means "transformative." I now know I was tinkering around the edges and avoiding the heart of the issue. If I really wanted to address the problem of low student engagement, I had to take a risk. I had to transform my paradigm.

So, in Spring 2009, I made a drastic change in my History of Women in Art class. I stopped lecturing in class. It was a frightening feeling to imagine spending 16 weeks with my students without lectures to deliver. Lectures are how I was taught art history and it's the only way I had ever taught it (in a physical classroom). What would I do with my students? What if they didn't participate? What if they didn't do the work? There was only one way to find out.

I revised my syllabus to communicate my student expectations and I carefully wrote a new class philosophy that emphasized the central role of community. I explained that a community is based on giving and taking and students would learn greatly from one another's contributions. I also communicated our new model to my students *before* the semester began. I expected that my innovative model might not appeal to some students so I sent out an email a week prior to class starting (using my course management system), attached the syllabus, and included a personalized letter explaining my intent and how the class would differ from a "typical" college lecture class.

As I created the plan for the semester, I found myself adopting much of the instructional design of my online class. The course was organized into modules that lasted one week on average. Each module included "pre-class," as well as "post-class" assignments. The pre-class assignments were due prior to the first class meeting for that particular learning module. They included: a description of the unit, a list of learning objectives, a reading assignment, a lecture—which I shared as an illustrated PDF and an enhanced podcast (my voice narration synced to still images), giving students a choice as to which one to access—and a VoiceThread.

The pre-class VoiceThread served a couple of purposes. First, it was a formative assessment. I designed it around prompts that were aligned with the learning objectives for that particular unit. The students needed to complete the reading and lecture to be able to make meaningful contributions in the VoiceThread—again, given a choice—in either voice, text, or webcam video format. The formative assessment gave students an opportunity to summarize and apply what they had learned from the reading and lecture. But each VoiceThread was also a participatory environment. Students were required to access the activity and leave a specific number of comments but they were also able to listen to and read comments left by other students, creating a contextual framework in which students could learn from one another.

Prior to the first class meeting for each new learning module, I spent about 45 minutes in my office listening to and reading the comments left in the VoiceThread. Traditionally, this would be time I'd spend preparing to deliver a lecture. Instead, I was assessing my students' understanding of core concepts and mentally preparing myself for an hour and a half of discussion and activities. As I reviewed the VoiceThread, I took detailed notes as I listened and read—I made charts that listed outstanding student contributions, identified topics that were mastered by the group, and highlighted areas that needed additional attention or held potential for deeper discussion. Then, when class started, I turned on the computer and projector and displayed the VoiceThread, which is simply accessed through a link in our course management system, on the screen. I referred to my notes and began to facilitate a discussion about the VoiceThread contributions—pulling individual students into the conversation, by name. This naturally took the class into a thoughtful dialogue, providing me with ample opportunity to applaud outstanding student work, prod students with Socratic questioning about comments that needed further explanation, encourage students to make deeper connections and engage in debate when conflicting ideas surfaced, and, ultimately, use the class time to fulfill the needs of the group and spend more time fostering critical thinking skills.

In addition to facilitating the VoiceThread discussions in person, I spent most of the rest of our class time having students work in groups to analyze and discuss image comparisons—the quintessential art history summative assessment that engages higher order thinking skills that can be challenging for students to foster with little to no opportunity for practice. We also debated, discussed, and questioned topics together, referenced relevant current events, took a field trip to a local woman artist's studio, and watched a full-length feature film about the life and art of 20th-century painter, Alice Neel (which was our only truly passive in-class learning experience . . . but was followed by a very emotional discussion fueled by the strong sense of community fostered in the group).

The post-class assignment in each learning unit included a second, unique VoiceThread that was designed around a second set of prompts that demanded higher order thinking skills. The slides in these VoiceThreads were more heavily focused on image comparisons in which students would be asked to contribute unique ideas, as well as build off of the ideas of students who commented before them.

Throughout the semester, there were also three summative assessments which involved a long take-home essay that required students to select from one of several prompts focused on comparing and contrasting two images and an in-class multiple choice and short answer test.

At the end of the semester, I conducted a simple survey using the survey tool within Blackboard—77% of students responded. I also invited students to my office to discuss their experiences. Three students came to speak with me and, with their permission, I recorded our 20-minute discussion (which has been shared on my blog ever since and is shared as a link in the book's online resources, see final chapter).

The survey results revealed increased student satisfaction, engagement, sense of community, and critical thinking. Despite the fact that 81% of students strongly agreed or agreed that the flipped classroom model required them to spend more time on homework assignments, 97% strongly agreed or agreed that the class was a successful learning experience. Additionally, when comparing the new flipped model to a traditional lecture class, 81% of students strongly agreed or agreed to the following: the new model was a more enriching learning experience, they had more opportunities to ask questions in class, their ideas and perspectives mattered more, and class-time was more relevant to their needs. Also compelling is the fact that 89% of the students who responded strongly agreed or agreed that the flipped classroom experience required more critical thinking than a traditional lecture class.

While from afar, it may seem that technology is at the core of the flipped classroom model, I would argue differently. The foundation of success is a clearly structured instructional design model that organizes content into learning modules, each aligned with a series of measurable learning objectives and a continued focus on modeling the importance of community. Also critical is the need for an instructor to make the intrinsic shift from "sage on the stage" to "guide on the side," or, to reference Barr and Tagg again, from an instructional to a learning paradigm.

College students are trained to expect a classroom environment that is designed around a hierarchy that places them at the lower level and their instructor above. This implicit structure informs everything about the way a student relates to the class—where they sit, how they prepare, and their attitude about the semester. Think about the physical organization of a classroom—desks organized around a single expert, sometimes even in an elevated "theatre" style. The messages that are implicit in the physical organization of a typical college classroom must be deconstructed for a flipped classroom to be successful.

Therefore, when an instructor embarks upon an instructional model that assumes a flattened relationship between student and instructor, like the flipped model, this must be communicated and discussed so it's clear to students. The "sample class philosophies" shared in Chapter 1 are an effective first step for setting the tone. But the success will rely upon consistent activities in and out of class that model a community of learners who are expected to share and learn together.

The flipped classroom opens the door to new possibilities for college learning models. It puts students in control of their learning and also gives them a chance to learn how they learn. As one student in my class responded, "I honestly thought that I would not like . . . it, I thought it would just add more work. After completing the course, I think that it actually helped me more than hurt me . . . I truly think that it has helped me learn better."

And that was the unexpected outcome of the class, for me. Originally, I began integrating audio podcasts and PDFs for lectures in my online classes in an effort to keep my content ADA compliant—so deaf students could have the option to read. But what I didn't realize was how valuable these options were to *all students*. Amazingly, at the end of the semester, when I surveyed my students I learned that when they were given the option to read or listen to a lecture, 40% chose to read, 15% chose to listen, 30% did *both* at the same time, and 15% toggled between the two throughout the term. Now, take a step back and think about those statistics. In a traditional college classroom, a student's only option is to listen—yet when given a choice, it was the *least utilized method*.

For me, this experiment illuminated a whole new way of thinking about college teaching. It has encouraged me to rethink our age-old ways of doing things and understand that our technologically rich society holds opportunities for making learning more effective, more inclusive, more engaging.

Problem or Opportunity?

I have shared my personal story with you to provide a practical example of how emerging technologies can be used to transform college learning but also as a way of reframing the student engagement "problem." It's true that today's students *are* different but they've changed only because of the deep-rooted shifts that have occurred outside the walls of our campuses. Technology should *not* be integrated into college learning for the sake of using cool new tools to engage tech-savvy students. Beyond the boundaries of our college campuses, technology is the driving force that has shifted our society to a highly collaborative, participatory model. And, within our classes, using it in support of a course's learning objectives is one way we can make our students' learning more relevant, more supportive of diverse student needs, more engaging, and prepare them for a successful life in our digital, interconnected, collaborative society.

By no means is my "flipped classroom" an example of the *best* way to modify our teaching practices with emerging technologies. Rather, it is offered as a *possible* way to change the course of college learning. Sometimes we can feel the need for a change but it's not until we "see" an example, that the ideas start to flourish and new paths open in front of us.

This chapter serves as our first step into the depths of a rich, complex topic. Each reader of this book has his or her own objectives and it is my hope that this book will meet them, in addition to pique your curiosity to try something new and inspire you to see new technologies in a new way. As the lives of our students continue to be transformed by social, mobile technologies, we have uncharted territory in front of us. As we struggle to fend off the distractions of Facebook and texting in our classrooms, in an effort to sustain our traditions, are we missing something grand? Something dazzling? We will never know if we don't pause and reframe our problems as opportunities.

The following chapters will provide you with more practical strategies through a cascading array of "showcases" from real college classrooms emphasizing how emerging technologies are reinventing college learning. As noted earlier, this book defines "emerging" as technologies that have made a splash in college learning but have not yet been adopted into mainstream teaching. The professors showcased in this book represent the diverse realities of college teaching. They come from 2-year and 4-year institutions, some with no instructional support, some with a robust team. Some teach full-time and others teach part-time (sometimes at more than one institution). But what they all share is the willingness to step outside their comfort zone and take a risk to improve a problem. Teaching with emerging technologies involves stepping outside the traditional guise of subject-matter expert and taking on the role of a learner.

The next chapter will provide you with several key strategies and techniques for making the shift to a student—centered class including writing your class philosophy and establishing the foundations of a community-oriented learning environment. From there, in Chapter 2 we'll continue to investigate the paradigmatic shift from teaching to learning and discover strategies for evaluating emerging tools; in Chapter 3, we'll peek inside the "essential" toolkit that is a must for all professors using emerging technologies for teaching; in Chapter 4, we'll examine audio and video tools for bringing your human presence into your online course content; in Chapter 5, we'll review participatory tools for collaborative learning and producing student-generated content; and, in Chapter 6, we'll consider the stunning effects of mobile learning on higher education.

SHOWCASE

To view a Google Site that includes a robust collection of resources accounting my flipped classroom experiment including a video overview of the model, video excerpts of the VoiceThread formative assessments, the student results, and the complete student interview, visit the online resource site at http://www.teachingwithemergingtech.com.

Chapter 1

Building a Solid Foundation

One semester, after I had recently integrated the use of a private Ning social network (see Chapter 5) into my online art appreciation class, I had a student come to me with an unexpected concern. That concern was an important moment for me, as it made me think more carefully about how my use of new technologies affected each student in different ways.

The semester was in its first few days and most of the students had already joined our network and were enthusiastically sharing photographs on their personal page—ranging from family vacation photos taken at the Louvre to pictures of their families and pets. I excitedly lurked in the network and enjoyed reading the student-student dialogue that was prompted by the photographs—"Hey, I went there on a family vacation too. When were you there?" or "Your dog is adorable. He looks like a dog I used to have" or, my favorite, "I remember you! You were in my geography class last semester!" I think about these early personal communications in an online class as being the early whispers of community building—kind of like the chatter and pre-class conversation that occurs in a hallway or in a classroom before the instructor begins a lecture.

But the student who came to me with a concern wasn't so keen on the idea of interacting with her peers in our social network. In fact, she sent me a thoughtful email explaining that she "isn't a teen-ager" and doesn't have any interest in being part of a class that resembles something like MySpace (this was pre-Facebook). That email changed my understanding of what it means to teach effectively with emerging technologies. It made me think more inclusively about who my students are and how their own experiences contribute to the way they learn. While my younger students generally jumped in enthusiastically to the Ning network, my older students weren't yet engaged in social networking and were suspicious and unsure about how it could correlate with a college class.

It was important for me to take this concern seriously. First, I was pleased that she felt comfortable enough to bring it to my attention and realized there were probably other students who might be compelled to drop a class, rather than engage their instructor in a discussion about the learning environment. Second, I realized that her reluctance was an effect of me being ineffective in how I contextualized the technology into my class and introduced my expectations to my students. This chapter provides strategies that will help ameliorate student concerns like the one I've shared here.

Supporting Student Success

For a moment, shift your viewpoint and think about your class(es) from the perspective of your students. Most of them register for classes to fulfill requirements and know very little about the actual class (expectations, requirements, etc.) until the class begins—that is, perhaps other than what they read on RateMyProfessors.com. Really, what happens when a student begins a class is that she enters a learning environment. The first time she sets foot in that environment, she begins to understand what is expected of her, what the experience will be like, and what her role in the process will be. And, more than likely, she is simultaneously registered for several other "environments" that will each be distinct. It's up to her to navigate these environments successfully and this can be a tricky—even daunting—task.

Now imagine being that student and having each of those learning environments shift *unexpectedly* throughout their duration. Unexpected shifts in a class are like unexpected turbulence on an airplane. They are uncomfortable, and stressful. Teaching with emerging technologies can be like flying with unexpected turbulence—if they aren't integrated into a learning environment effectively.

While today's traditional college-age students are more comfortable with experimenting with new technologies than previous generations, they aren't necessarily fluent with all tools, nor do they understand how to use them to be productive, lifelong learners—which, I believe, is a skill that all college classes can contribute to developing. Moreover, college classes are comprised of generationally diverse groups of students. You'll have students, much like my apprehensive student, who become anxious at the prospect of taking a class that integrates technologies they've never used. The key to supporting the success of *all* your students is to start students off on a solid foot the moment a class begins. Implementing the strategies outlined in this chapter will ensure your students are clear, from the start, about *why* you are requiring them to use tools in your class, *how* the tools will enhance their experiences, as well as what is appropriate and inappropriate behavior and content.

As you integrate emerging technologies into your classes, strive to communicate the following items in your course syllabus and share it with your students on or before the first day of class:

A. List of Tools That Will Be Used and Your Reason(s) for Using Each

Upon entering a class, students should have an opportunity to preview the supplemental tools you plan to have them use. This does not imply that you cannot use a tool not shared on the list; it's merely an effort to communicate your plans to students so they have a clear picture of the road ahead.

As noted earlier, sharing this information with students *before* the start of a class, even before they register for a class, is ideal, as it empowers students to be able to register for classes that meet their own learning styles and overall preferences. Today, we have many students who are enthusiastic about using mobile apps or social media in a class, but, at the same time, we also have four different generations of students on college campuses now, as well as students with disabilities that may be challenged by using particular tools and others that may be supported more effectively in a rich media environment. Considering the student experience is an essential part of teaching effectively with emerging technologies.

With that said, students also want to understand *why* you are using the technologies. This is important to share for two reasons. First, because it illuminates the connection between learning (the student's goal) and technology. Sadly, only about half of college students feel that their professors use technology effectively.[1] So, don't expect your students to feel excited about using a new tool or two until you can lucidly demonstrate why it's relevant to their success. Second, hearing your explanation may turn a reluctant baby boomer with little to no technology skills into a curious learner who is ready to try something new. And this can be an empowering experience for both the student and the instructor.

Here is a sample I've written:

> *In this class, you will create your own blog using blogger.com, a free and easy-to-use open blogging platform, owned by Google. A blog is a website that is similar to an online journal. You will regularly add new entries or "posts" to your blog in response to required readings and class discussions.*

> *Creating your own blog will provide you with your very own website to examine, analyze, and discuss the written works we will read in our class. You will find that blogging is quite different from writing a paper and submitting it to your professor for a grade. Your blog will be shared with your peers and the rest of the world, placing your unique ideas and perspectives in a collective, living, and global dialogue about our topics.*

> *Your blog will extend you the opportunity to connect with people around the world who are reading the same books, receive comments from authors, and your blog may inspire ideas for other bloggers. At the end of our class, you will have a living product that will remain active after the end of the class.*

B. List of Required Supplemental Equipment

What equipment do students need to possess (or have access to) for your class? Most colleges and universities have basic technology requirements that are communicated to online students prior to registration (computer, browser, high speed internet connection). If you are teaching a face-to-face or hybrid class with emerging technologies, it's critical to establish a similar toolkit—this may be something already established and shared on your campus or it may be up to you to get this conversation initiated.

In addition to the tools and equipment needed to access your class, however, you must also clearly communicate the equipment students will need to contribute to your class. This may include:

- webcam (for participating in video web-conference or recording video presentations in YouTube);
- microphone (for having audio conversations over the internet during office hours, recording an audio presentation, leaving a voice comment in a discussion,

interviewing an artist in Mexico, recording a variety of opinions about a current event);

- digital camera, smartphone or other mobile device that can take digital pictures (to document a field trip, identify a biological specimen, share examples of local architecture that demonstrate influence from ancient civilizations).

C. Access Expectations and Resources

In your list of required supplemental equipment, it may be more appropriate to encourage students to "have access" to the tools, rather than require them to be purchased. Be sensitive to your overall student demographic. Many colleges in lower socio-economic regions will find that using emerging technologies for teaching and learning can create financial hardships for students. And the technologies students possess really varies by their income level. For example, students who come from a low socio-economic background could be more likely to possess a smartphone than students who come from a moderate income level. This is because more middle-class income groups have had access to the internet via broadband, while lower class income groups have not been able to afford access to the internet at home and, therefore, have acquired a smartphone to bundle phone and internet access. Don't let "access" prevent you from innovating; rather, view it as an important reason to collaborate with your colleagues to find creative solutions to the hurdles you identify.

Frequency

When you share your list of equipment, explain how frequently students will be required to use a webcam or microphone—or whether the use of these tools are options (options are an excellent way to accommodate students with learning or physical disabilities and support students' diverse learning preferences). Some students may not have their own webcam, for example, but may be able to make arrangements to use a family member's or friend's.

Campus Access

Also, is the equipment available for student use on campus? You may need to do some research in this area. Visit your campus computer labs or reach out and contact the appropriate campus representatives. If the answer is "no," it's important for you to share the need for these resources with your colleagues involved with planning efforts. Today's typical college or university provides students with access to internet equipped computers but, in the future, it is likely to include private audio and video recording stations, as well as mobile lounges in which students can check out mobile tablets for completing course assignments. Also, keep in mind that some campuses still block the use of social media sites in computer labs. If you are having your students interact in a Facebook group, view or share videos on YouTube, or engage in a chat on Twitter, then you will need to ensure your students have access to these sites from computer labs on campus.

Discounts or Special Pricing

Are the tools you are encouraging your students to use available in your campus bookstore or through an online partner at a discounted rate? For example, the Foundation for California Community Colleges has developed "College Buys," an online portal that provides discounts on software and hardware to students, faculty, and campuses. If you are aware of resources like this, be sure to share them with your students (and your peers!)

D. Necessary Software

Will your students need to download and install or use any applications to complete class assignments and projects? For example, if you are sharing a podcast with your students, will the episodes be accessible on a regular website or will they need to download and install iTunes? If you are using a program that runs on Flash, it's likely that, today, all students will have Flash on a laptop but if they're planning to access your class via an iPad (or other iOS device like an iPhone or iPod Touch), that will be a problem, as these devices do not currently support Flash.

Providing this information to students ahead of time will allow them to make alternative access plans. Also, it's a good idea to encourage students to upgrade to the most recent version of the applications on your list. Include a direct link to the website(s) when possible.

E. Supplemental Mobile Apps

While it's not yet appropriate to assume all students have a smartphone or a tablet in their possession, it's a great idea to share a list of mobile apps that students could use in support of your class. More and more emerging technologies are developing mobile apps to complement a user's experiences and extend them into a continuous access model. Keep your eyes peeled for the "mobile" icon throughout this book to identify emerging technologies that may be used with mobile devices.

F. Examples

You will have many students who are not familiar with the technologies you've identified so it's always a great idea to include a link to an example of a podcast, a wiki project, a collaborative mind map, etc. Seeing an actual example will relieve a student's anxiety and start to help him understand what to expect more clearly. You may also consider including screenshots of the environments in your syllabus.

TIP

Use Jing for Easy Screenshots and Screencasts

There are many ways to create screenshots and screencasts (videos of your computer screen). My favorite tool is Jing. It's free, runs on both PCs and Macs, and produces .png files that can easily be annotated and saved to your computer and screencasts that can be shared online via a free Screencast.com account or downloaded and then shared within a course management system or website. See Chapter 4 for further discussion.

G. Student Perspectives

It's amazing how much more relevant advice is to a student when the advice is shared by another student. Our society has swiftly evolved into a participatory culture, placing peer reviews at our fingertips before we dine at a restaurant, vacation at a hotel, or buy a book. Students want to hear from other students about what they should expect in a class—and that desire is the fuel behind the popularity of RateMyProfessors.com.

SHOWCASE

Wisdom Wall

Figure 1.1
Screenshot of
Wisdom Wall.

Last semester, I asked my departing History of Still Photography students to leave some advice for you to help you be successful in this class. Here is what they said!

Here is a creative, fun, and easy way to use a Google Doc to share past student perspectives with incoming students and start to build community in your class. In my classes, students are provided with a link to the *Wisdom Wall* at the beginning of each class. The Wisdom Wall is a collection of advice contributed by students from the previous term.

I am consistently impressed by the advice the students share with each other and, honestly, learn a great deal from the comments myself!

Sample Wisdom Wall Contributions

"It may seem like a lot of work at first but just breathe and try not to get overwhelmed as this class is very rewarding. Just be sure that you keep up with your blog posts on Ning and do your VoiceThreads and you will do great!"

"Don't be afraid of all the technology. The teacher is really good about showing you step-by-step how to do everything and after a while it gets easy and starts to become fun."

"If you are dreading this class listen up! Michelle makes this class so interesting and exciting. You will be learning and enjoying the class before you can say yuck . . . Ning is a little class community that will allow you to interact with fellow students. This class was awesome!"

"The main advice I can give is DO NOT GET BEHIND . . . If you choose to procrastinate you will not be happy with the results because things pile up quickly and unexpectedly."

How to Create a Wisdom Wall

Coordinating the Wisdom Wall can be a very simple process or it can be a time-consuming task. One option would be to have students email their "advice" to you and then you'd be responsible for curating a display of the feedback on a website or in your course management system. At the end and beginning of a new term, there are many other, more important, tasks for you to focus on. So, empower your students to be able to create the Wisdom Wall on their own!

Here's an easy solution: create a free Google Doc (see Chapter 5 for more information) and customize the sharing and edit settings so the webpage can be updated by your students. In essence, selecting the following settings transforms a Google Doc into a wiki page:

1. Set the "Sharing Settings" to "Public on the web" or "Anyone with the link" (the latter ensures that the content will only be visible to those who have access to the link and it will not appear in Google searches).
2. Adjust the "Edit Access" to "Allow anyone to edit (no sign-in required)."
3. Leave clear instructions at the top. I prefer to say, "Click in the white space below the red horizontal line and type your advice to my future students." Then insert a simple horizontal red line below the instructions.
4. If you prefer, create a fun graphic and insert it at the top of your Wisdom Wall. I created the graffiti text in Figure 1.1 using The Graffiti Creator (http://www.graffiticreator.net/), took a screenshot of it, saved it to my computer and then uploaded it into my Google Doc.
5. Paste the link to the Wisdom Wall Google Doc in your course management system and encourage your students to leave their advice before a particular time and date.

Building Community

The mainstream use of social technologies like Facebook, YouTube, Flickr, and Twitter has transformed learning outside the college classroom into a rich, community-based experience. Each year, more and more traditional college-age students enter our classrooms with an intimate understanding of the relevance and value that participatory learning provides. As Cathy Davidson and David Goldberg noted in *The Future of Thinking*:

> Since the current generation of college students has no memory of the historical moment before the advent of the Internet, we are suggesting that participatory learning as a practice is no longer exotic or new but a commonplace way of socializing and learning. For many, it seems entirely unremarkable.[2]

Participatory learning simply "looks" different from traditional college learning. In most college classrooms, learning relies upon the successful transfer of information from a subject-matter expert (professor) to receptacle (student). This traditional model expects students to play a passive role in learning. In contrast, participatory learning situates individuals within a fluid community in which members make contributions by sharing ideas of their own and responses to the contributions made by other members. Those contributions are commented on by other community members, leading to further dialogue, refinement, growth, and debate. The intermeshing of community members in a participatory learning environment is grounded in clear "community guidelines" that are a stipulation of joining the community.

Michael Wesch's 2011 video, "'The Visions of Students Today' 2011 Remix One," a compilation of student-generated videos submitted in response to Wesch's call, conveys experience of 21st-century college "learners" who are immersed in traditional lecture classes, wondering what their peers are thinking and feeling like their opinions and thoughts are irrelevant, even locked out from the process of constructing knowledge and understanding.[3] To me, the video (a still from which is shown in Figure 1.2) illustrates the relevance gap between our mainstream teaching pedagogy and the effects of our students' participatory learning experiences outside the walls of college.

Integrating emerging technologies into your college classroom does not necessarily mean you will transform your class into a participatory learning community. But it does extend this opportunity to you and it's a concept that you should think about as you begin to experiment and understand the technologies you will employ. For those professors who wish to create a community-based learning experience for students, it's

Figure 1.2 Video still, "My space in the room" by Derek Schneweis. Used with permission.

necessary to realize that you will need to explicitly frame your class in this way from the very first day of class and then cultivate a learning environment that fosters and encourages trust, student contributions, peer comments, and the overall collaborative construction of knowledge. This vision of learning should inform the decisions you make about tools to use in your class.

A. Class Philosophy

A brief description of the type of environment your students should expect. Each college professor has his/her own style. Communicating how you approach your class and the role that emerging technologies play will encourage students to be more productive. But the most important element of a class philosophy is making a commitment to modeling it throughout the semester. A philosophy is only words on a page—the time your students spend in your class will infuse it with meaning.

Sample Class Philosophy From One of My Online Classes

This class is a community. We all have the same objective: to learn. Online students often feel isolated but it's important to know you are not in this alone! I need each of you to approach our online class with a great attitude and a willingness to help each other. Many problems and questions can be resolved by asking a fellow student. I am always here to help you but I truly believe your experience will be better if you communicate with your fellow students throughout the semester. The technologies woven into this class will increase your ability to share, connect and learn from one another.

Sample Class Philosophy From One of My Face-to-Face Classes

This is not a typical "lecture" class. In "lecture" classes, students come to class and passively receive information delivered via lecture format. Throughout the semester, you will be completing regular web-based assignments outside of class. This will include the class lectures which will be shared in two formats: audio podcasts and PDFs. Rather than using class time passively, you will actively participate in critical analysis, discussion, and debate as we apply the ideas from the mobile lectures. Your full commitment to the format of this class is critical to your success.

Every person in this class is part of a community focused on learning. Throughout the semester you will be expected to help each other and you will learn to rely upon each other. You will treat each other with respect and should always feel comfortable approaching one another for help. I will do everything in my power to create a trustworthy, stimulating, active learning experience for you. As your instructor, I am here to facilitate your learning and guide you each step of the way. I am also here for you to discuss any problems or challenges you are having. Please don't ever hesitate to contact me via email or phone or visit me during office hours.

My role is dependent upon having a group of individuals who are committed to being here for every class and being ready to contribute keen insights and perspectives to our discussions. We are in this together! This class will not be a success if you do not hold up your end of the bargain. Deal?

B. Community Groundrules

Communities thrive through the active contributions of their members. Students need to feel safe and perceive their learning environment as a trusted space to share and collaborate with their peers. Developing a clear set of community groundrules and sharing them with your students is imperative. Aside from developing the set of rules, it's critical that you weave them into the use of the participatory tools you'll be using. Agreeing to the groundrules could be made a condition of participation, for example, and/or you could share your groundrules on a website (a simple Google Doc will do for those of you without knowledge of html or a process for hosting your content) and link to it from the assignments you share in your course management system. Essentially, keeping the groundrules at the surface of your students' participation is important, as this approach serves to remind them of their expectations and also provides an opportunity for you to communicate how students should deal with violations. The groundrules empower students to play a central, rather than peripheral, role in their learning.

Sample Community Groundrules

A community is a group of individuals who work together to support a common goal or interest. We are working together to support the successful achievement of our learning outcomes. In an effort to ensure our community develops, thrives and sustains throughout our time together, the following groundrules will be in effect at all times.

- Treat contributions made by other members of the class with respect.
- Reach out and help when you see the need. And ask for help when you need it.
- Back up your contributions. As with any content you share online, keeping an alternative copy is essential. Each community member is responsible for keeping a back up of his/her contributions.
- Have patience and a sense of humor with technology. There will be hiccups, expect them.
- Keep an open mind. If you're feeling reluctant, that's ok. Take it one step at a time and look at this as an opportunity to learn something new.
- Contribute regularly to collaborative activities to ensure other members of the community have ample opportunity to read/listen, reflect, and respond to your ideas.
- Respect the diverse opinions and viewpoints of each member of our community. Differences allow us to learn and grow together.
- Understand that communications shared through text have a higher likelihood of being misinterpreted than the spoken word. Therefore, when you type a thought or a comment, read it carefully before you submit it. If you question the way it is worded, read it out loud to yourself. If you still question the way it's phrased, re-write it.
- Contribute regularly to group dialogue, including blog posts and replies. The contributions of each individual play a role in the collective strength and diversity of our community.
- Members of our community are to be restricted to enrolled members of our class, in an effort to maintain a safe, trustworthy discussion environment.

- All image and video content shared within this community will reflect acceptable content standards. You are expected to use discretion and, if asked, you will be expected to demonstrate how your content supports the theme of our community: "[enter a description of the community's theme here]."
- Understand that any network member has the ability to create a new forum in our network. However, s/he who creates the forum immediately takes on the responsibility of moderating it. This means you have committed to regularly responding to new comments and greeting new members of the forum or group.
- If, at any time, you feel that any of these groundrules have been violated by a member of our community, you are encouraged to bring your concern directly and immediately to [enter professor name], our community leader. Clearly identify which groundrule has been violated and include specific evidence of the violation in your email. Your concerns will be addressed promptly with careful consideration in an individualized manner.
- After this class is over, your access to this community will end. If you share content that you'd like to preserve, it is your responsibility to make a back-up of it before the class ends.

Empower Students to Prepare Prior to the Start of Class

Emerging technologies provide many options for professors and institutions to increase a student's readiness for the start of a new term. Our newly participatory society has crafted higher expectations for understanding precisely what an experience will be like before it begins or before a purchase is made. When I visit Amazon.com to purchase a book, for example, I read the reviews left by other users before I make my decision. When my 10-year-old son wants to purchase a new toy, he goes online and reads the reviews left by parents and other kids to decide whether or not it's worth his money or if the advertisements are just a slick persuasive tactic. When I'm traveling, I'll pull out my smartphone and check the reviews of a restaurant on Yelp before I decide to dine there. Our participatory society has empowered us as consumers to be informed and make choices that are tailored to our preferences, needs, and expectations before we make a decision to take the plunge.

Unfortunately, things don't work this way in the world of higher education. But I like to imagine how different things would be if they did. Now we can easily make the argument that students *want* to know about their professors and the expectations that will be placed upon them after registering for a course. This desire is easily confirmed by considering the wild popularity of RateMyProfessors.com. At the time of writing this, the site boasts that it shares more than 11 million student-generated ratings of over one million professors. And the site receives roughly two million page views a day.[4]

Trying to gain insight about a professor or a particular class is part of the age-old student experience. I know I made efforts to gain insight about my professors before registering for a class when I was in college and I bet you did too. But, imagine with me, if students had the opportunity to learn about you directly from *you*, rather than tap into what other students thought about you. Why don't we share our syllabi online for students to review prior to registering for a class? Why don't we record a video introduction and share it online so students can get a sense of who we are, the person they'll be spending 50 hours with over the course of a semester?

Web 2.0 era has empowered each of us to become content creators. We can now easily record video direct from a webcam into a free YouTube account and embed it on a website. And we are no longer barred from creating a website because we don't know html or because we don't have server space. There are many options available to us now.

If you like the idea of sharing your course expectations, syllabus, and other critical resources with your students before they register for your class but don't have the resources to develop a traditional website, consider creating a free site with Google Sites (discussed more in Chapter 5).

Your site may include:

- A welcome video recorded in YouTube and embedded on the site along with captions to ensure it's accessible to students with hearing impairments.
- Your course philosophy, demonstrating your teaching style and high level expectations for the students.
- A Tech Toolkit with links to necessary software the students may need to download or equipment they will need. For example: a PDF reader, iTunes (if you're using iTunes U), Flash, a USB microphone, a webcam. Include links to the software and links to examples of the equipment they will need so they can be prepared and ready to learn on day one.
- The syllabi for your class(es). Early access to a syllabus provides students with the ability to discern many important elements to support their success. For example, if it's a class that is delivered online but requires a face-to-face component that is not possible for a student, s/he can decide ahead of time not to register. If the workload for the class is more intense than expected, s/he may decide to take the class another semester when there are fewer personal commitments to contend with.
- A message to students about using the site for a continuity planning in case a disaster occurs. If a college campus is shutdown due to an earthquake or a Blackboard server goes down due to a flood, students need to know how to stay in touch with you. The Google Site provides you with a method to share important updates with students who may otherwise be left detached and unclear about the status of the class.
- Student perspectives. Capture feedback from your students as they leave your class and then share it on your site.
- Emergency plan. Include a notation on your website that identifies it as the vehicle you will use to communicate with your students in an emergency situation. This will reduce frustration, concern, and anxiety if your main communication tool becomes unavailable during the class.

SHOWCASE

Instructor Google Site Sample

Figure 1.3 Screenshot of instructor Google Site.

Figure 1.3 is a screenshot of a Google Site I created. It includes all of the resources in the list above. I've shared this site as a template in Google Sites which means it is available for you to copy and customize as your own. To learn how, visit the web resources for Chapter 1 at: http://www.teachingwithemergingtech.com

The Nuts 'n' Bolts of Teaching in the Open Web

The nuts 'n' bolts of how you integrate emerging technologies into your teaching will hinge partially upon your existing technological infrastructure. What is the central access point for your students outside of your physical classroom? Most institutions these days provide professors teaching online, hybrid or face-to-face classes with access to a course management system or CMS (Blackboard, Moodle, etc.), while other professors independently use eLearning resources provided through a publisher or have a simple website or blog on which they share links to web-based activities.

A course management system (which may also be referred to as a learning management system or LMS) is a proprietary or open source software that contains some basic functions: an area for announcements, storing content in a hierarchic structure, traditional assessments (quizzes, exams), and a grade book. Additional functions vary by CMS (and version) but may also include blogs, wikis, ePortfolios, and web conferencing platforms.

Course management systems are excellent tools for organizing content into a clear, consistent learning path for your students. They provide a centralized location for sharing pertinent course materials with students who are registered for your class. CMSs also require students to authenticate so you are ensured the students who access the material you share are enrolled in your class, and they also provide options for tracking student log-ins, access to content, and participation. Student authentication supports the construction of a safe, trustworthy learning environment and the gradebook included with a CMS is an essential, secure portal for sharing private information with students.

But many college instructors today are less than thrilled with the tools commonly included in a CMS toolkit for delivering awe-inspiring learning and, therefore, experiment with the wealth of web-based, social technologies that allow for easy content creation and sharing. This section will touch upon three important elements to keep in mind as you integrate emerging technologies into your students' learning:

- Embedding vs. linking;
- Student privacy;
- Using copyrighted material for teaching.

A. Embedding vs. Linking

Frequently, teaching with emerging technologies involves the integration of content from another website into your online course. When you integrate that content, it's important to think carefully about how to integrate it most effectively to avoid derailing the flow of your students' learning. Embedding content into your online class is like taking a pair of scissors, cutting the content out from the secondary webpage and gluing it onto a page in your course management system, eLearning portal, or website. Linking to content, essentially, appears as an active URL or hyperlinked text on a page. Clicking on the URL link or hyperlinked text opens a new window or tab, displaying an external webpage to view and interact with the content you've shared with them.

Embedding content from other websites is an effective way to keep your students focused on the content inside your main access portal, rather than fragmenting their experience by going out to multiple websites. You may find it helpful to realize that many students who are sent out to another website get sidetracked and don't come back to the class. (Can you relate? I know I can!) Identify whether or not embedding the content in your primary content portal is an option. If it is, is the embedded version effective or is it best to provide both the embedded and linked version? Here are some things to keep in mind.

Is Embedding an Option?

Most Web 2.0 tools provide the option to embed content elsewhere, but it's important to be sure. To check, look for a "Share" or "Publish" option within the tool you are using; this is typically where you'll find the "embed" option, if it exists. If you see an embed option, the site will provide a string of "embed code" which is a snippet of html code that a browser interprets and, in turn, displays a "cutout" of your web-based content. The code you copy will specify the dimensions of the embedded object. Some sites provide different size options. When selecting a particular size, you'll want to be sure it fits within the display area of your course (this is a process of trial and error). When you locate the embed code, highlight the entire string of code and copy it to your computer's clipboard. (To copy on a PC, press Control + C. To copy on a Mac, press Command + C.)

Locate the Visual Text Box Editor

You can easily embed content in a course management system, eLearning portal or webpage. The key is locating the visual text box editor. Many experienced CMS users are not aware of this option. The visual text box editor is a function within a course management system that is usually made available to users by default but I have seen some instances of institutions who disable this feature. Visual text box editors will vary in appearance but it should look something like the one shown in Figure 1.4.

Provide Supplementary Information About the Content

Before you paste your embed code in the visual text box editor, it may be a good idea to introduce the content you are embedding (if you haven't already done this somewhere else). If it's a video you are embedding, type a simple link in the text box that introduces its topic and tells students how long it is. If it's a video without captions, you may provide a link to a transcript for students who require this accommodation.

Figure 1.4 Screenshot of visual text box editor 1. Reproduced with permission from Moodle.

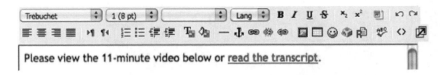

Figure 1.5 Screenshot of visual text box editor 2. Reproduced with permission from Moodle.

Toggle to HTML Source Code View

This is a critical step. Before you paste the embed code into the text box, you must switch from rich text mode (which shows text the way it will appear to your students) to html source code view. How to do this varies but usually the action is performed by clicking on a button that looks like this "< >" or you may see a button or tab that says, "HTML." Click on the appropriate icon and then paste the code into the blank space below the existing text.

Save

Click the necessary buttons (save, continue, etc.) and you should now see your embedded object below the supplementary information.

B. Student Privacy

For centuries, college learning has occurred in a physical space partitioned from the rest of the world by four walls. The idea of encouraging or requiring students to interact with each other and share their work in digital format in the public web challenges

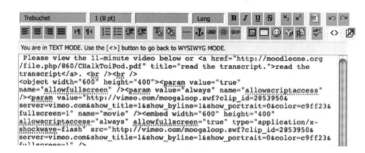

Figure 1.6 Screenshot of visual text box editor with embed code. Reproduced with permission from Moodle.

Figure 1.7 Screenshot of embedded video.

the traditional paradigm of college learning in many ways. And frequently this change ushers in some alarming concerns about student privacy. Being concerned about the privacy of your students is certainly important but what's more important, possibly, is that we, as educators, provide opportunities for our students to learn how to responsibly participate in the online environment. This is a critical 21st-century skill that much of the population does not yet possess. Using emerging technologies in your college classroom is an opportunity to foster this relevant skill. Teaching effectively with emerging technologies requires you to facilitate meaningful, safe interactions in support of your students learning—which is nothing new. How to achieve this objective with emerging technologies is new. Here are some things to consider.

Identify the Tool-Specific Privacy Settings

As you evaluate tools for adoption in your teaching (which is the focus of Chapter 2), you'll want to spend time exploring the privacy options that are provided. Many tools will extend the option to share the content in different ways that may range from public in the open web, retrievable through a web search; to private, requiring sign-on or password; and anywhere in between. For example, I use a web-based tool called VoiceThread to foster participatory learning activities designed around images (for more information, reference the Introduction, as well as Chapters 4 and 5). When I create a VoiceThread, it begins as a completely secure environment. For example, if I were to send the link to anyone else, they could click on it but they'd only see a message indicating that they don't have privileges to view it. I can easily make adjustments to this default setting by allowing "anyone" to view it (which actually means "anyone with the link," but it won't be found through a web search) or I could choose to have it included on VoiceThread's "Browse" page, making it fully public. Similarly, if I share a video on YouTube, I have the option to mark the video "Public" (for anyone to find and view), "Unlisted" (which means it will not be found through a web search and will not appear in searches in YouTube but will be viewable by anyone who has access to the link), or "Private" (which requires me to type in the email addresses of the individuals who have my permission to view the video. This option requires the permitted users to sign-in before viewing the video).

Select the Best Security Setting

The "best" security setting is not always the most secure. You need to think carefully about the environment you wish to cultivate with the content and manage your workload effectively. If you select the most secure option, you are going to be entering many emails (possibly hundreds, depending on how many students you have and how much teaching support you are provided) and, undoubtedly, dealing with many students who encounter log-in challenges. Frequently, the mid-range option is a great option, particularly if you are teaching in a course management system. If you copy the link to your content and share it within your course management system, then students must first authenticate to view and interact with the content. This doesn't make it impossible for the content to be shared outside of class but it does reduce the likelihood of this occurring and eliminate the concern of having others find the content within a web search and leave comments that may be disruptive, inappropriate, or symptomatic of spam. With that said, one of your objectives may be to have your students participate in a global conversation about a particular topic. Perhaps you want your students to be able to invite others to contribute to the course dialogue or you want them to have the opportunity to experience receiving commentary from the global community. If this is the case, then you may want to consider a fully public option and encourage your students to become effective monitors of spam and foster the ability to ferret out inappropriate contributors (both essential 21st-century skills.)

Inform Students About Who Their Audience Will Be

Don't expect students to intuitively understand who will have access to the content they contribute for your class. Be sure to explain this to students prior to their participation. If you are having students participate in public web-based activities, it's a very good idea to encourage them to sort through information that is appropriate to share. A good rule of thumb is to encourage students to abstain from sharing personal information about themselves and focus on fulfilling the course-related prompts and assignments.

Develop a Student Use Agreement

Develop and share a student use agreement in your syllabus and have students verify their acceptance through a written contract or by completing an automated "syllabus quiz" in your course management system in which they "accept" the agreement. This practice clearly informs students about the parameters of the environment you have constructed and also provides you with tangible verification of their acceptance of the parameters, providing practical protection for both you and your students.

Offer Options

Be prepared to offer students options about how they represent themselves online. Here are some suggestions to consider. Encourage students to use their first name and last initial when sharing contributions. Be creative with avatars. Some students may not feel comfortable sharing a photograph of themselves. Encourage them to share an icon or image of something that represents who they are.

Provide Accommodations When Necessary

Be aware that there may be students who have valid privacy concerns about sharing contributions online. For example, I once had a student who was taking online classes because she had a restraining order against her husband and was afraid to leave her house. It's important that you create an environment in which students, first, have an opportunity to share these concerns with you and, second, have alternative options that allow them to contribute and learn along with the rest of the class in a safe, trust-worthy environment. One strategy is to allow the option to use a pseudonym, with your approval, to preserve the anonymity of these students. But keep in mind that pseudonyms can complicate the assessment process, as you will need to identify the author of the anonymous content.

Do Not Share Grades

Student grades should always be kept private and shared in a secure environment that requires a user authentication, like a course management system. Email is not considered secure.

TIP

Download these Student Privacy Tips in a handy PDF from the Chapter 1 resources shared online at: http://www.teachingwithemergingtech.com.

C. Using Copyrighted Material for Teaching

Copyright is one of the most complex and dizzying topics in academia today. Our digital, internet culture has flipped the logic of copyright on its head and, as a result, copyright restrictions are becoming increasingly more stringent and teaching with digital materials is becoming more bewildering. Questions about the legality of using copyrighted material in your classes (in analog or digital form) should be brought to your respective campus representative(s). Individual colleges and institutions should have their own individual copyright policy to assist with guiding faculty through these muddy waters, and protecting their own interests. The information provided here is offered for educational purposes and is not intended to replace the advice of your campus representatives or serve as legal advice.

Understanding copyright in its historical context is a good place to start our conversation. In 1787, the writers of the U.S. Constitution included a clause in Article 1, Section 8 (arguably a sign of its significance) that has shaped the copyright laws we live with today.[5] The clause was guided by the interest to preserve the public's right to access knowledge without being limited by a creator's right to restrict access: "The Congress shall have Power To [. . .] promote the Progress of Science and Useful Arts, by securing for limited Times to Authors and Inventors the exclusive Right to their respective Writings and Discoveries."[6]

It may seem contradictory to understand that copyright law exists to *promote* public access to knowledge when, from my experiences, many professors today live in fear of being slapped with a lawsuit for violating copyright law. For the owner of the copyright has the exclusive right to govern who may use the work only after receiving express written authorization from the copyright owner to do so. This fear often prevents educators from sharing content that contains copyrighted works, even when their distribution of the materials may fall well within Fair Use (see description on following page). When copyright of a work expires, the work enters the public domain and may be used, at that time, without authorization. However, understanding when a work enters the public domain isn't so easy (and varies by country).[7]

Fair Use

The Fair Use clause of copyright (section 107) further supports the interest of promoting public access to knowledge by permitting the use of copyrighted material without the permission of the copyright owner for certain purposes (including teaching, scholarship, and research). But to determine whether a particular use of a copyrighted work is fair, four factors must be considered.

- The purpose and character of the use, including whether such use is of a commercial nature or is for non-profit educational purposes.
- The nature of the copyrighted work.
- The amount and substantiality of the portion used in relation to the copyrighted work as a whole.
- The effect of the use upon the potential market for or value of the copyrighted work.

(Title 17, Section 107 United States Code)

So, with this information clearly spelled out, it should be simple to identify whether or not a particular use of a copyrighted work for teaching, scholarship or research falls into fair use, right? Well, it's not. And digital content makes this process more ambiguous, as the definition of a "copy" is no longer clear-cut. In fact, you will never be able to ascertain a hard "yes" or "no" to whether or not a use is fair. What's critical is that you understand the four factors of fair use and are able to apply them with good judgment in your own teaching, following your institutional guidelines (which, for example, may provide a more clear definition of what your college/university has determined to be "the amount and substantiality of the portion used"). There are also some very helpful tools that have been developed to assist with this process. If a copyright owner feels that you have overstepped the boundaries of fair use, there may be the need to address how the use of work applies to each of the four factors.

Open Licenses

Creativity in the 21st century is deeply informed through remixing which involves a process of using existing material to create something new. Remixing, a product of our digital society, deeply informs contemporary creative expression and you'll find examples of it on YouTube, Flickr, Twitter, and other social media outlets. In remix culture, "fair use is your friend," as the Center for Social Media has so eloquently argued in its clear and informative video shared about video remixing.[8]

But, as movies are now recorded daily with mobile phones and other devices and shared directly to YouTube and unattributed photographic images are downloaded and redistributed on other websites, it becomes increasingly difficult to ensure the content one shares does not include copyrighted material. For example, if I were to take out my phone and record my niece jumping for a balloon and I happen to record a popular song playing in the background, I would violate copyright law. Now that's probably not going to be an issue if I keep that video between me and my family. But when I click the "Share to YouTube" button on my phone and publicly share it with the world, that's a different story. No, I didn't intentionally use copyrighted material without the permission of the copyright owner but, nonetheless, I did and that's a violation of the law. Why is this really such a big deal? Well, imagine if I were a documentary filmmaker who captured a copyrighted song in the background of a key interview. I could be required to pay thousands of dollars in royalty fees for the licensing rights to use that song—which would directly undercut my creativity, as well as the progress of filmmaking in general.[9]

While instances like these continue to wreak havoc on the logic of copyright law and the tenuous balance between the rights of authors/creators and public access to knowledge, there is some relief. Thanks to some creative and progressive thinkers, there are now several license options that copyright owners may choose to apply to their original works (without releasing their rights under traditional copyright law). These new, flexible options are referred to as "open" licenses. When a copyright owner applies an open license to his work, it clearly specifies how and under what circumstances another person may use the work *without permission*. As public knowledge and understanding about open licenses continues to spread, more and more copyright owners are applying open licenses to their work and, in turn, there is an increasing supply of content that is easily accessible and may be redistributed and remixed without the anxiety of a looming lawsuit. Further, the energy stimulated through the use of open licensed content is fostering a culture of sharing that, arguably, in the 21st century promotes public access to knowledge more so than traditional copyright.

Creative Commons

One of the most popular open licenses today is Creative Commons (CC). Founded in 2001 with support from the Center for the Public Domain, Creative Commons has grown to support projects and licenses for works in more than 70 jurisdictions.[10] Creative Commons has become the "global standard for sharing across culture, education, government, science, and more."[11] To gain further clarity about how Creative Commons licenses work, it's helpful to think about them as a license option that falls somewhere between traditional copyright and the public domain, as illustrated in Figure 1.8. A work that is shared with a Creative Commons license clearly specifies how and under what circumstances a work may be used without the permission of the copyright owner. These conditions include one or more of the following: attribution (giving credit to the copyright owner), no derivatives (the work must be shared unchanged and in its entirety), share alike (new creations that use the work must be shared under an identical license), non-commercial (the work may not be used for commercial purposes).

Creators can easily discern which license is best for their work by using the Creative Commons *License Chooser*.[12] Licenses may be applied to digital works through the inclusion of an image of the license and websites containing digital works may embed

Copyright
All Rights Reserved
Re-use requires permission from
the copyright owner.

Creative Commons
Some Rights Reserved
Use is allowed without
permission *under the conditions*
noted in the license.

Public Domain
No Rights Reserved
Use is allowed without permission,
as there is no copyright owner of a
work in the public domain.

Figure 1.8 Permisable use of Creative Commons licensed works.

a snippet of html code into the page which allows for the content to be found and used more easily.

As an educator utilizing emerging technologies for teaching and learning, understanding the value that sharing brings to our culture is critical. Learning, after all, doesn't occur without the sharing of knowledge. As you move forward with the creation of your own content in digital form, consider applying a CC license to your work and play a role in changing the world.

HOW TO FIND CREATIVE COMMONS LICENSED WORKS

Creative Commons is largely based upon community participation and works that utilize a CC license do not enter a database that can be accessed and searched directly. However, there is a portal page that will connect you with several useful content searches that will assist you with locating pertinent CC-licensed content. Keep in mind that it is your responsibility to ensure the content you find through a search on the following portal is, in fact, shared through a CC-license.

1. Go to the Creative Commons Search portal at: http://search.creativecommons. org.
2. Click on one of the options that aligns with the media type you are seeking: Flickr (image), YouTube (video), Jamendo (music), SpinXpress (media), etc.

TIP

Downloading Images From the Web Is Easy

If you are on a PC, right mouse click on the image and select the "Save Image As" option from the drop down menu. If you are on a Mac (and don't have a right mouse click option), press "Control" and click on image. Then select the "Save Image As" option from the drop down menu and save the image file to your computer.

TIP

A Simple Way to Keep Track of Image License Details

I use Flickr a lot to find images for use in my digital work. I have found that it can be very easy to forget the name of the author and keep track of the license type of each image after I download them to my computer. I have found it useful to save the image with a filename that includes the author name and the details of the license. For example, a photograph of a yellow flower by John Catskill with an Attribution-No Derivative-Non Commercial license would be saved as, "YellowFlowerByJohnCatskillAtt-ND-NC.jpg"

TIP

Use Google Chrome's Picnik Extension to Manage the Attribution of Images

As you become more acclimated to teaching with emerging technologies, you will want to experiment with different browsers. Using a different browser is kind of like changing your shoes—it feels different but you can still get around fine. Browsers can be customized with add-ons or extensions, some of which are available for all major browsers and others aren't. Google Chrome, for example, has an extension available called Picnik which is not available in Firefox, Safari, or Internet Explorer. In 2011, Picnik was acquired by Google and now you need to be a Chrome user to get your hands on its great features.

I like using Picnik because it's a simple way to edit an image online and gives you the ability to include the attribution on the image itself. Doing this prevents the need to add text to a presentation, website, etc., to attribute the author because it's already on the image itself. Making the attribution separately isn't terribly difficult but it is easy to forget or lose track of the author's name, so add it with Picnik! Note: if the image you've selected was shared with a "No Derivatives" specification, you will violate the license by appending the author's name to the image.

Learning From Student Frustrations

At the start of this chapter, I shared a story about a student who was reluctant to engage in the social network I had integrated into my class. After that student reached out to me, we engaged in a dialogue—I listened to her concerns and responded with more context, explaining why I had integrated Ning into the class, shared comments from previous students about how it had helped them stay connected and engaged, and encouraged her to keep an open mind. In our exchange, I made it clear to her that the *only* thing she was *required* to do in the network was become a member and write a weekly blog post in response to prompts I provided in the corresponding learning modules. That was key to her success. After she had more clarity about what she was required to do and what was optional (the sharing of pictures, for example), she felt more comfortable in the social, participatory environment Ning offered.

It was clear to me that this was a high risk student who may drop the class and, for that reason, I stayed in close contact with her throughout the first few weeks of class. By week three, she had turned the corner and began contributing some very compelling reflections in our weekly blog post assignments. And by the end of the class, she shared something priceless with me. She wrote me an email in which she thanked me for listening to her concerns and reflected on the class as a successful learning experience. But there was one more thing she shared that, to me, stands out as one of my most memorable teaching moments. She told me that, for the first time in her life, she felt connected to a culture from which she had previously felt excluded. My class gave her the opportunity to learn what a "social network" was and how a "blog" works—these were words that were meaningless to her before. Whereas, before the class she felt marginalized from the technological landscape surrounding her—viewing it as a space for "teen-agers"—after the class she felt included and welcomed. And, here's the best part—she was a teacher who has began using emerging tools in her own classes.

Chapter 2

A New Paradigm for a New Century

Steve Hargadon, creator of Classroom 2.0 and the host of The Future of Education podcast series, illustrates the effect of our 21st-century life, peppered with Web 2.0 and social media tools, as a massive wave.[1] If you take a moment to imagine the image of a large wave in your mind, the way you naturally construct your vantage point may communicate how you feel about emerging technologies, as well as your level of current participation. Do you picture that wave about to hit shore and destroy everything in its path? Are you cautiously watching it from a protected balcony? Or are you riding it, shrieking with excitement as its energy throws you off balance?

Riding the wave with expertise surely isn't everyone's objective but if you're reading this book, you clearly have some interest in submerging yourself a bit further. Typically, one of the most overwhelming elements of teaching with emerging technologies is deciding which tool or tools you should try. Note that I say, "try." Teaching with emerging technologies is, by nature, experimental and failure is an implicit step in an

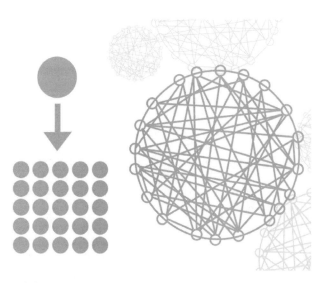

Figure 2.1 Lecture and participatory learning models. Image by Laurie Burruss. Reproduced with permission.

experiment. If we don't fail, we don't learn, and if we don't learn, we won't improve upon what we're already doing. And in the 21st century, improving upon a centuries-old tradition of teaching and learning is critical.

Still, failure is tough. And professors don't openly relish the opportunity to fail. Why would we? Professors are products of an educational society that has taught us to discourage failure, to be ashamed of mistakes, to always be right. Grades are presumably evidence of successful learning and that relished 4.0 grade point average certainly doesn't include room for any failures at all. Low grades follow students, tarnishing their GPA and reducing their opportunities to apply for scholarships and other merit-based achievements and opportunities. The modern educational system and, in turn, western culture defines failure as something bad that should be avoided at all costs.

Ironically, brain research tells a much different story. Take a moment to reflect on something you are good at—cooking, painting, gardening, computer repair, fishing, negotiating, debating—anything. Think back to your experiences over the years, as you grew and developed your skills and expertise in this area. First, you wouldn't have had a chance to develop your skills only through reading about how to be proficient in this skill. You had to actively participate and give it a try. And as you reflect back on your growth, what was it that enabled you to improve? It was probably a new dish that tasted horrible, a color combination that looked garish, a computer screen that didn't go on when it should have, the big fish that got away, a lost deal, a failed argument . . . you get the picture.

Now you might agree with that point when we consider it in the context of personal hobbies or everyday skills, but what about in your teaching? What motivates you in your role as a college instructor? How do you view your role in a classroom? Is it important to you to see your students succeed? Each college instructor will respond to these reflective questions differently and your response will provide valuable insights about your teaching paradigm.

Barr and Tagg's insightful article from 1995, "From Teaching to Learning," explores the characteristics of two distinct paradigms that operate in various ways throughout higher education: the teaching paradigm and the learning paradigm. Applying these ideas to your own classroom is an illuminating experience, as it encourages you to examine your teaching values and philosophy.

I find it helpful to imagine Barr and Tagg's instruction and learning paradigms at opposite ends of a continuum. Take a moment to review a few of the characteristics of each paradigm listed in Figure 2.2, reflect on your own values and motivation and identify where on the continuum your teaching lies.

Emerging technologies hold an array of opportunities for teachers committed to achieving the outcomes of a learning paradigm. By nature, social media, Web 2.0 tools, and mobile apps are participatory and easy to use. In short, they create a cascading array of opportunities for students to be active contributors in the learning process, yielding fabulous ideas for assessments and strategies for increasing student interaction.

It's also a good practice to identify where on the continuum the institution(s) at which you teach lies. Institutions demonstrate their priorities through policy and decision-making. And, often, an instructor who values the priorities of a learning paradigm but teaches at an institution committed to the instruction paradigm finds oneself in a challenging situation.

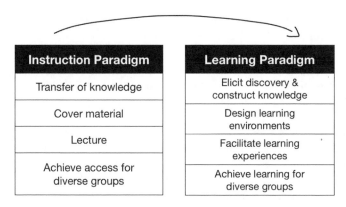

Figure 2.2 Instruction and learning paradigm charts.

I shared the Barr and Tagg model in a presentation I gave to a mostly-faculty audience at a very large, public university and the Twitter backchannel (a stream of real-time, brief messages sent by audience members from mobile devices in response to my presentation) included comments from instructors that questioned whether or not their institution would ever embrace the learning paradigm. The evidence they cited for this was the large size of their classes. The more students there are in a class, the more challenging it is to adopt the priorities of a learning paradigm. For example, designing a learning environment in a philosophy class that is targeted at eliciting discovery, constructing knowledge, and achieving specified learning results for a diverse student group requires an instructor to engage with students, have an understanding of who the students are, have a willingness to adapt and shift the direction of activities in response to the group's unique needs, make necessary accommodations for special needs within the group, and make an effort to arrange course content in a variety of ways including text, image, and video. The more students there are in a class and the more classes an instructor teaches, the more difficult it is for an instructor to master the learning paradigm, regardless of his or her personal teaching preferences and values.

But be creative! There are practices in motion that demonstrate how emerging technologies can introduce more active learning into even very large lecture classes. For example, Perry Samson, who teaches Atmospheric, Oceanic & Space Sciences at the University of Michigan and was named Michigan Distinguished Professor of the Year in 2010, uses a product called LectureTools which transforms his students' laptops and smartphones from a classroom nuisance to a learning tool.

After logging in to LectureTools, Samson explains:

> [S]tudents can 1) type notes synchronized with the lecture slides; 2) self-assess their confidence in understanding the material being discussed; 3) pose questions for the instructor and/or teaching assistant; 4) view answers to questions (with questioners' names removed) as posed by the teaching assistant during or after class; 5) select and enlarge the slide, draw on it (cross-platform on Mac or Windows) and save the drawing; 6) respond to instructor's questions; 7) view podcasts, if any,

that are uploaded by the instructor after class; and 8) print the lecture slides and notes for off-line review.[2]

Moreover, these activities are all contained in a cohesive learning environment-rather than scattered across multiple files and sites—that is archived and can be viewed by students after class has ended to aid in the preparation of exams.

LectureTools offers many of the perks of "clickers," a type of first generation "student response system."[3] But when given the choice between using clickers or LectureTools, 90% of Perry's students would choose LectureTools because, as one student explains, "LectureTools is very easy to access and use, and provides a multitude of note taking options, unlike clickers."[4] Emerging technologies often open new opportunities for creating environments that students can customize to their own needs, which directly increases engagement and motivation.

What changes has Samson identified in his student interactions? Well, more students are asking questions, which can be a tremendous challenge in large lectures. In a semester, about half the class asked at least one question and 17% posed at least one question on five or more days.

As products of our educational system, professors have traditionally been positioned as the experts with all the answers. Experimenting with new technologies in your teaching will require you to step into a new teaching paradigm that encourages and fosters a community of learners who are incentivized to work together and solve problems.

So, expect to fall off that surfboard a few times as you begin to teach with emerging technologies, but view each of those slips as opportunities to grow and cultivate more effective, relevant learning experiences for your students.

The Value of Participating

Ana Maria Slingluff-Barral started her career as a research scientist. After many years working in the private sector, she walked away from her title and security to teach college biology classes. It didn't take long for Ana to realize how scarce full-time community college positions are and see that her new life, at least for the interim, was going to involve teaching classes at a variety of colleges and universities.

During Ana's transition, she found herself feeling as if she had lost her identify. She went from a formal title and institutionalized role to being affiliated with several colleges, not feeling like part of the "full-time" community at any of them. In an effort to improve her teaching, she registered for a face-to-face workshop at a local community college that was offered to teach instructors how to use Camtasia, a popular tool that records and edits screencasts (videos of your computer screen). That face-to-face workshop gave her the skills to create video lectures that she could use to web-enhance her biology classes. But it also piqued her curiosity about technology and teaching and gave her the self-confidence to try new things.

Not long after that, Ana enrolled in my *Building Online Community with Social Media* class. This is a fully online class I teach for the @One Project, the same program that funded Ana's Camtasia workshop. @One is funded by a grant from the California

Community College Chancellor's Office and offers professional development classes designed for community college instructors but widely used by K-12 and higher ed faculty from across the nation. In the class, instructors experiment with an array of social media tools and work together in participatory environments to discuss and evaluate how the tools can be applied to online classes to foster a sense of community among learners. The first interaction I remember having with Ana was the week the participants were asked to create a Twitter account and start tweeting. She wrote to me expressing concerns about privacy and social media. In our exchanges, we talked through those concerns and I told her she shouldn't do anything she isn't comfortable with, but I wanted her to give it a shot. My advice was simple-don't share anything private (advice every user of social media should take to heart). Soon thereafter, I saw her first tweets surface. They continued with more and more frequency through the end of the class.

In the months that followed, Ana used Twitter to share resources she stumbled upon but also to follow research biologists, organizations, and educators around the world, many of whom followed her back. Quickly, her social media participation enabled her to curate her very own global network of users with shared interests. This Personal Learning Network (PLN) has changed Ana's life. In a recent Skype conversation with her, she shared that even though she continues to teach at several institutions, she no longer feels isolated. She has found a sense of community, a feeling of belonging—but also has a dynamic network of individuals who she exchanges relevant teaching ideas and resources with and leans on for help or advice about teaching-related problems. You can visit Ana on Twitter at: http://twitter.com/Bio_prof.

But tweeting wasn't Ana's only venture into the world of social media. She also became a blogger. She uses her blog as an open space to work through teaching experiments—writing about her ideas, summarizing her experiments, and then reflecting on how things went. Like her post, "From Boring to Blogging, Part 3," in which she shared her newly created rubric for scoring her biology students' reflective blog posts that captured the scaffolded development of their research. Her blog has opened her teaching process to the world, allowing anyone to learn with her through her journey into teaching with emerging technologies.

I asked Ana how her teaching has changed, since she first embarked upon her use of Twitter. She said she feels like her teaching has transitioned from "black and white to full color." "When I teach now, I feel like I am serving my students a buffet rather than a quick bite to eat." She reflected on the ways that social media and Web 2.0 tools have potential to engage more students and extend confidence to learners who are traditionally marginalized through lecture and exam-oriented classes. "More of my students feel good about themselves."

But this transformation has not been without challenges. Ana is interested in encouraging her students to use their mobile phones to take pictures in their lab and use the images for web-based blogging and other assessments but one department she teaches in has a strict policy against use of cell phones in class. As a part-timer, these institutional policies are difficult to negotiate. In higher education, there are many traditionalists who do not see the value of turning a phone into a learning tool. Like psychologist Abraham Maslow said, "If you only have a hammer, you tend to see every problem as a nail."

As a veteran researcher, Ana shared some intriguing perspectives about the broader implications of social media in the field of research. She noted, "We used to just have peer-based research journals to share our findings. Today, we still have them but social media provides us with a space to experiment with global input. My blog and my Twitter users play a role in helping me work through my problems and learn from my failures. In the end, everything will be kicked up a few notches. It's exciting." Ana was recently tapped by Carnegie Mellon to participate in a national review of an open online biology course. She sure has found her place.

Social media transforms teaching from static delivery of content to an ever-changing practice. The only way to learn this is through experience. Participating with emerging technologies outside your classroom is the best way to see the array of possibilities they hold. And, taking a page of advice from Ana, I agree that finding a face-to-face workshop is an outstanding way to get your feet wet.

Getting Started

After you have experientially learned the potential that emerging technologies hold for your students' learning, you'll want to understand how to get started with integrating them into your teaching. This chapter provides a list of criteria for evaluating individual tools for use in your own teaching. But before we dig into the evaluation criteria, there are a few critical elements you should flesh out to eliminate messy surprises down the road.

Take some time to reflect on the following questions.

I. What Function Will the Tool Serve in Your Class?

Identifying the function the tool will serve is essential and stresses a critical message about teaching with emerging technologies: a tool should always be used *in support of* pedagogy.

This first step may be difficult and, honestly, you may not have a crystal clear response to it at first but you are likely have some idea. Take some time to reflect on this question and even write a few paragraphs about how you envision your students' experience or your teaching approach to be enhanced or altered by an emerging technology.

Three common functional uses of emerging technologies in learning are:

1. Enhancing interaction between you and your students and/or between students themselves. (See Chapter 4.)
2. Creating online content for your class; for example, online presentations, demonstrations, lectures. (See Chapter 4.)
3. Creating a learning activity that integrates student-generated content and/or participatory learning. (See Chapter 5.)

If you are seeking a tool to facilitate a learning activity, you should keep some solid groundrules in mind about instructional design:

- Start with clear, measurable learning objectives.
- Select a tool that accommodates your objectives and is appropriate for the tasks or skills to be learned.
- Align your use of the tool with these objectives.
- Develop a rubric to assess your student's work.

II. Who Will Use the Tool?

Will the tool be used exclusively by you (for example, to create communications for your students or lecture content), or will students also use it (to create their own presentations or interact in a peer-to-peer learning environment, for example)?

If students will use the tool, you should plan to do the following.

Provide How-To Instructions

Clear instructions must be developed and shared with students from the start. These may, very well, already exist. Don't hesitate to share online instructions with students, especially if they're provided on the tool's website.

Part of teaching with emerging technologies is responding to frequent updates and redesigns of tool interfaces and new enhancements. Therefore, relying upon external help resources will lighten your load. You should only develop your own instructions to enhance and refine existing instructions. Think ahead, anticipate changes, and build a plan to save yourself time.

Also, search for instructional "how-to" videos in YouTube (you will likely find more than you imagined!) or consider creating screencasts (covered later in this book) that provide visually illustrated steps of how to use a tool. If you create screencasts, consider breaking up the process into short 1–2 minute steps, rather than one long "how-to" video. This enables students to focus easily on the step they have a question about and also facilitates easier updating later on.

Finally, consider sharing the content you develop on your blog, website, YouTube, Twitter, etc., with a Creative Commons license. Give back to the community that helps you.

Explain the Purpose

Along with "how-to" instructions, explain to students *why* you have integrated this tool. How will it enhance their learning? How will it enable them to increase their communication with you and/or their peers? As noted in Chapter 1, students appreciate understanding the context of a new tool when they are asked to use one.

Build in Opportunities for Student Feedback and Use Results to Make Improvements

At the end of the course, survey students to evaluate how effective their learning experience was with the tool. Did it achieve the function or objective you had in mind? A scale combined with open-ended questions is an effective approach to measuring the effectiveness of the tool.

TIP

Google Forms for Quick and Easy Student Surveys

A Google Form (an option packaged within Google Docs, see Chapter 5 for more information) is a useful tool for many reasons. First, it's a quick, intuitive, and free option for crafting surveys with visually pleasing themes that can be shared easily via a link, email, or embedded on a website. Second, the responses are compiled in real time into a Google Spreadsheet for easy viewing and evaluating. Responses can be viewed line by line in the online spreadsheet or you can view a visual summary of them if you prefer. You also have the option to copy an existing template, shared by a Google Doc user, and customize it for your own use.

Figure 2.3 shows two questions excerpted from a live "Google Form" Student Survey.

Figure 2.4 shows a few responses to these questions in Google spreadsheet format.

Figure 2.5 is a summary view of all the responses to the same two questions.

To create a Google Form, you must have a free Google account. Log into your account, select "Documents," click on "Create New," and select "Form" from the dropdown list. Also note the "From template" option at the bottom of the list. Creating a new form from an existing template, shared by another Google Doc user, saves you time! Get started with Google Forms at: http://docs.google.com.

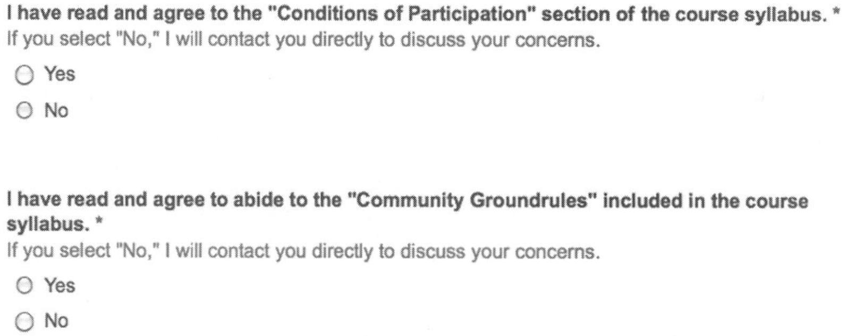

I have read and agree to the "Conditions of Participation" section of the course syllabus. *
If you select "No," I will contact you directly to discuss your concerns.

○ Yes

○ No

I have read and agree to abide to the "Community Groundrules" included in the course syllabus. *
If you select "No," I will contact you directly to discuss your concerns.

○ Yes

○ No

Figure 2.3 Google Form screenshot.

I have read and agree to the "Conditions of Participation" section of the the course syllabus.	I have read and agree to abide to the "Community Groundrules" included in the course syllabus.
Yes	Yes
Yes	Yes

Figure 2.4
Google Form spreadsheet view.

I have read and agree to the "Conditions of Participation" section of the the course syllabus.

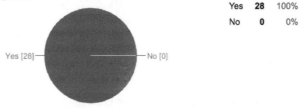

Yes	**28**	100%
No	**0**	0%

I have read and agree to abide to the "Community Groundrules" included in the course syllabus.

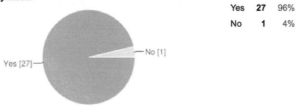

Yes	**27**	96%
No	**1**	4%

Figure 2.5 Google Form visual view.

SHOWCASE

Here is an example of how Julia Parra, Assistant Professor at New Mexico State University, uses Google Docs for pre- and post-assessments of her students to assist her with effectively integrating Web 2.0 tools into her classes to promote effective online student collaboration and groupwork.

She has students complete the pre-assessment survey to identify if her students own or have access to mobile devices (and which ones), as well as media technology like a webcam, video recorder, or audio recording device. She also assesses the students' self-perceived strengths (I am often the leader/editor/researcher in a group, I am good at creating multimedia, I am good at creating web-based media).

Parra leverages this information to implement group work and particular tools that best support the student group. She is able to organize the students into groups more effective by evenly distributing the self-identified leaders, editors, researchers, multimedia and web specialists.

At the end of the term, she implements a post-assessment to evaluate how the selected emerging technologies were at supporting collaboration, as well as gathering the students' overall satisfaction with the tools.

Figures 2.6, 2.7 and 2.8 are screenshots of Parra's post-assessment survey.

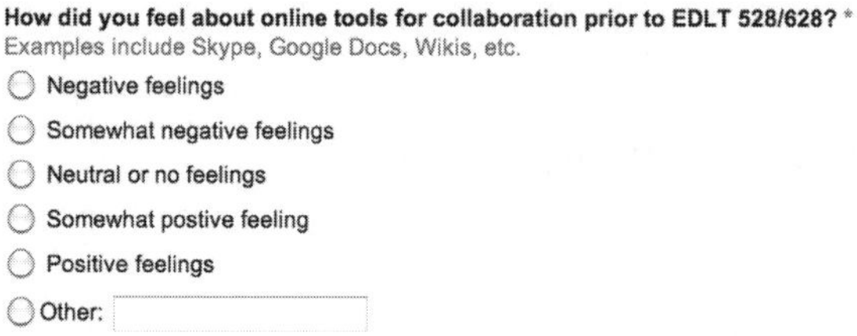

How did you feel about online tools for collaboration prior to EDLT 528/628? *
Examples include Skype, Google Docs, Wikis, etc.

◯ Negative feelings
◯ Somewhat negative feelings
◯ Neutral or no feelings
◯ Somewhat postive feeling
◯ Positive feelings
◯ Other: _____

Figure 2.6 Parra screenshot 1. Reproduced with permission from Julia Parra.

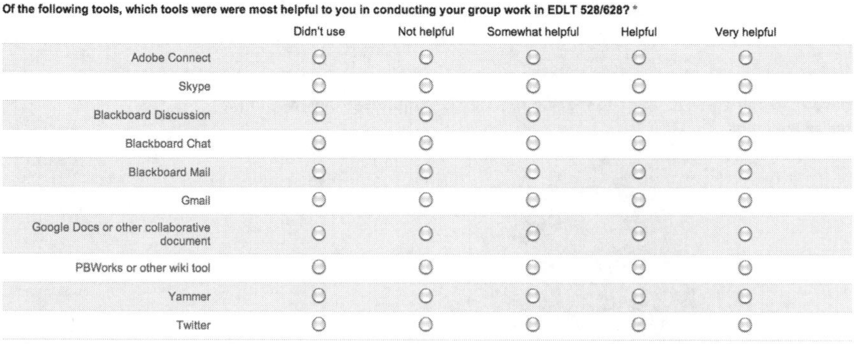

Of the following tools, which tools were were most helpful to you in conducting your group work in EDLT 528/628? *

	Didn't use	Not helpful	Somewhat helpful	Helpful	Very helpful
Adobe Connect	◯	◯	◯	◯	◯
Skype	◯	◯	◯	◯	◯
Blackboard Discussion	◯	◯	◯	◯	◯
Blackboard Chat	◯	◯	◯	◯	◯
Blackboard Mail	◯	◯	◯	◯	◯
Gmail	◯	◯	◯	◯	◯
Google Docs or other collaborative document	◯	◯	◯	◯	◯
PBWorks or other wiki tool	◯	◯	◯	◯	◯
Yammer	◯	◯	◯	◯	◯
Twitter	◯	◯	◯	◯	◯

Figure 2.7 Parra screenshot 2. Reproduced with permission from Julia Parra.

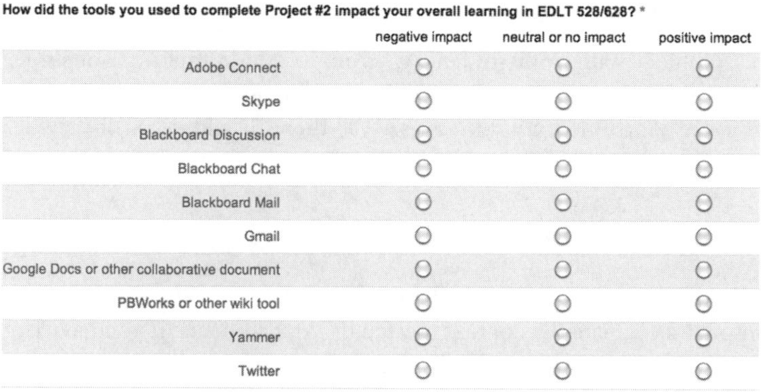

How did the tools you used to complete Project #2 impact your overall learning in EDLT 528/628? *

	negative impact	neutral or no impact	positive impact
Adobe Connect	○	○	○
Skype	○	○	○
Blackboard Discussion	○	○	○
Blackboard Chat	○	○	○
Blackboard Mail	○	○	○
Gmail	○	○	○
Google Docs or other collaborative document	○	○	○
PBWorks or other wiki tool	○	○	○
Yammer	○	○	○
Twitter	○	○	○

Figure 2.8 Parra screenshot 3. Reproduced with permission from Julia Parra.

When asked how the results of the survey were used in support of future online classes, Parra said:

> [The results of this survey] confirmed my belief in the importance of the process that I have formally developed and implemented in my online courses. I have always supported my students with the development of technology skills and provided some scaffolding for group work. However, the more formal process that I have developed is supportive in my overall process of online course design and is something that I can share with others.

And Parra is committed to sharing with others! In fact, if you'd like to view and/or use her surveys, you may do so. She has shared both of them as a template. Just go to the links below, and select the option to "use this template."

- Student Pre-Assessment: http://goo.gl/unijj
- Student Post-Assessment: http://goo.gl/NpxEA

(Both of these links are also included in the Chapter 2 online resources, accessed at: http://www.teachingwithemergingtech.com. See the final chapter of this book for more information.)

III. How Will Your Workload Be Affected?

Encouraging students to create content with a Web 2.0 or social media tool is an effective way to assess learning, create relevant learning experiences more likely to foster deep learning, and develop critical thinking skills.

But if you are planning to have your students create content with social media or a Web 2.0 tool, plan ahead to ensure you have a clear understanding of how your workload may be affected. Here are some things to consider.

Your Participation Level

Effective, regular contact with your students is an important component of student success, especially if you are teaching online. Will your adoption of a new tool increase your need to actively contribute in your classes? Will there be additional areas where students may ask questions, for example, that you will need to monitor?

Class Size

The number of students in your class(es) will directly drive the amount of time it takes for you to monitor and evaluate the content created by your students. If you have large classes, think creatively about how you will assess the student-generated work.

Frequency of Assessment

How often will your students be using the tool? Weekly? Bi-weekly? Will you evaluate each student's work every time the tool is used?

===

TIP

The Nudge System for Grading Blog Posts

A blog is a terrific way to integrate reflective writing and other creative activities into your students' learning. But often professors feel overwhelmed by the need to grade every blog post. Here is a creative grading strategy that *may* help!

Let's say you assign a weekly blog post in three classes. Each class has 40 students in it. That means you have 120 posts to read and grade each week-on top of other duties. Rather than telling your students you'll grade the blog posts each week, schedule two dates in your term when the blogs will be graded—midterm and end of term work well.

Then, between the formal and comprehensive grading periods, inform your students that you will be active in the blogs each week after a due date. You will visit a handful of blogs and verify that they are current. If you identify a blog that is missing a post, you will leave a "nudge comment" on the student's blog. The nudge is phrased something like this: "Your blog posts are looking great but I am delivering a 'nudge' because you are missing our most recent post, [insert post title here]. We are all looking forward to seeing it soon!"

Each time a student receives a nudge, it is an automatic point deduction that will be incurred when the blogs are graded. It's a good idea to keep a simple list tally of nudges (perhaps on a spreadsheet used for grading notes). This is helpful just in case someone elects to delete your nudge comment.

The system worked well in my class. The deduction for a nudge was significant (5% of half the term's blog grade, so two nudges would drop a student an entire letter grade) and students who received nudges were very responsive and got back on track quickly.

===

Checklist for Evaluating Tools

After fleshing out your responses to the questions listed above, you may already be considering a few different tools. So, how do you decide which one to implement into your class? There is no magical answer to that but you will find that evaluating each tool against a set of criteria is a good practice to integrate into your workflow. The following checklist was inspired by Bethany Bovard's clean, useful "Web 2.0 Selection Criteria," which you can find at: http://tektrek.wordpress.com/2009/03/02/web-20-selection-criteria/.

I. Accessibility: Can All Students Access the Tool or Content?

- Is the tool accessible by Windows and Mac users?
- Is the tool or content viewable in a variety of web browsers?
- Does the tool work well for those with dial-up connections?
- Does the tool provide options that support ADA compliance?
- Does the tool have a mobile app (or plans for a mobile app) for a variety of devices (iPhone, Android, iPad, etc.)?

Ensuring your course materials are accessible to all students, regardless of learning preference or challenge, is an important priority for every instructor. In the United States, online course content must, by law, meet the criteria as outlined in Title II of the American with Disabilities Act, Section 508. When a face-to-face, hybrid, or online course utilizes static content (PDFs, Word docs, html pages, video files, etc.), the steps to fulfilling this criteria have been clearly established.[5] However, integrating emerging technologies into an online class can introduce quite a bit of murkiness, especially when those tools are being integrated with the explicit intent to foster learning through participation, rather than through the traditional, passive transfer of knowledge.

To understand the importance and value of accessible web content, University of Washington encourages you to consider the following:[6]

- Most individuals who are blind use either audible output (products called *screen readers* that read web content using synthesized speech), or tacticle output (a refreshable Braille device).
- Individuals with learning disabilities such as dyslexia may also use audible output.
- Individuals with low vision may use screen magnification software that allows them to zoom into a portion of the visual screen.
- Many others with less-than-perfect eyesight may enlarge the font on websites using standard browser functions, such as Ctrl + in Firefox and Internet Explorer 7 (Windows).
- Individuals with fine motor impairments may be unable to use a mouse, and instead rely exclusively on keyboard commands, or use assistive technologies such as speech recognition, head pointers, mouth sticks, or eye-gaze tracking systems.
- Individuals who are deaf or hard of hearing are unable to access audio content, so video needs to be captioned and audio needs to be transcribed.

- Four million iPhones were sold within their first 200 days on the market in 2007–08. iPhone users navigate the web using a small screen and touch interface on a device that doesn't support Adobe Flash.

The High Tech Training Center in California, which supports California's 112 community colleges, offers a helpful model for instructors to evaluate the accessibility of content and it lends itself nicely to emerging technologies. Their model delineates "Three Cs" of accessibility: Container, Content and Capability.[7] This model illuminates the multiple layers that need to be considered when evaluating a tool's ability to support all learners.

Container

Does the tool (i.e. the "container") support the use of assistive technologies (i.e. screen readers, text to voice dictation software, etc.)? If so, are there any features within the tool that do not support assistive technologies?

Content

Is content authored outside the tool and imported into the tool accessible to all (images, video, a mind map, etc.)? The accessibility of the content is separate from the container itself. And, as explained by Keegan and Brown, "While the container itself may not be fully accessible, the externally authored content can provide the information necessary for using assistive computer technologies."[8]

Capability

Is the container capable of supporting the creation of accessible content?
This evaluative step is a difficult one for professors, as it requires expertise that most professors do not possess. Individual institutions are responsible for establishing a process for course accessibility. This may involve professional development training opportunities, dedicated support, or a blend of these two. What's important is that you understand the resources that are available to you and that accessibility be integrated as a priority into the development of your course.

TIP

Web²Access (http://www.web2access.org.uk), a project of the University of Southampton in York, shares accessibility reviews of popular Web 2.0 and social media tools. The database of products that have been reviewed is robust but the reviews were conducted in 2009 and many tools have made substantive changes since then which will affect their accessibility rating (in a positive or negative way). Their ratings offer an excellent starting point for evaluating a tool's accessibility and the criteria they use for their testing is openly shared on their site, providing a valuable tool for institutions to initiate their own evaluations.

Be an Advocate for Accessibility

Finally, approach accessibility with an open mind and think outside the box. Some emerging technologies hold the potential to shift the paradigm of accessibility, creating new methods of reaching students through rich media. For example, to accommodate students who are deaf, educators are traditionally encouraged to share text-based transcripts of audio shared in an online setting. But what if we could, also, include a video of a person signing that auditory content? Signing is the natural communication method used within the deaf community. Imagine how empowering that experience would be for students!

In your work, if you identify that a tool has value to your particular discipline, but realize there are accessibility hurdles, don't run. Rather, reach out to your campus resources for support and advice about how to use it with accessibility in mind from step one. Also, reach out to the tool's developers and share your excitement and concerns. Engage in a conversation with them that offers an opportunity for them to listen and understand the needs of educators. You may or may not find them receptive to your needs and that will inform your thoughts about pursuing the use of the tool.

A Case Study: Emerging Technology and Accessibility

In 2007, I began experimenting with VoiceThread for teaching art history online. VoiceThread is a free, web-based tool that provides a secure, participatory environment for discussing media through text, voice, or webcam comments. I was drawn to it because I felt unable to effectively teach a visually centric discipline in a text-centric course management system. Unlike a course management system, VoiceThread organizes conversations around media, flipping the traditional dichotomy of text–image. And users (that is, students) are extended the option to leave comments in text, voice, or video, cultivating an inclusive participation experience.

The first semester I used it, I noticed a few things. One, when given choices, students select the method that works for their individual needs. For example, I had a dyslexic student who excelled in the discussions when she elected to use her webcam to make comments, yet struggled endlessly to convey her idea through text. Two, I was empowered to *really teach* my online students through the feedback I was able to leave with my webcam and microphone. Rather than reading all my feedback in text form, students were given an opportunity to see and/or hear me, which enabled me to convey my excitement, concern, or pride about their work.

Despite all this wonderful inclusivity provided by VoiceThread, the tool itself was designed in a Flash "container." While Flash is installed in most web browsers (making it readily available to nearly all online students), it does not currently support the use of screen readers, an assistive technology used by students who are blind. I began a dialogue with the VoiceThread developers about my concerns and they listened—we actually scheduled a phone call at one point with an accessibility specialist to gather further evaluation about the hurdles that the product would present to users relying upon screen readers. And three years later VoiceThread released VoiceThread Universal, a "back door" that provides access to VoiceThread content through an html, rather than Flash, container.

Experimentation and advocacy are important threads in the conversation about teaching with emerging technologies. Grass-roots education leaders are key to accessible emerging technologies.

2. Learning Curve

- Is the tool easy to use?
- Are help resources built in?

As you evaluate different tools, consider how challenging they are to learn. Reaching back to Chapter 1's focus, consider the student perspective. If students will interact in or create content with the tool, take extra caution in selecting tools that are intuitive. This will have a direct impact on the number of questions you receive. Seek out easy-to-use tools and evaluate built-in help resources. But also remember, there will always be a learning curve and your role is to motivate students, provide clarity about *why* they're using the tool, and point to clear instructions and help resources to support them.

3. Cost

- Is the tool free?
- Is there a premium version?
- Can your goals be achieved with the free version?

Free is always preferred—that goes without saying! And premium cloud-based technologies can offer phenomenal values through monthly or annual subscription rates. The days of expensive OS-specific software are behind us!

But as many start-ups have learned, "Free is not a business model" and you should consider that tools that offer both a free and premium services are demonstrating a more mature revenue model. This is a sign that they are more likely to be around for a while . . . but there are never guarantees! Also, keep in mind that service agreements with emerging technologies are likely to change over time. What's free today may not be free next year.

4. Authentication

- Does the tool require users to create an account?
- Is there an option to create a customized authentication integration with a course management system?

When a student is required to sign-in to an online account before making a contribution or creating content in a tool, anonymous contributions are not permissible. That's important to you, as you must be able to identify contributions made by students in order to assign points for work (if you have decided that's relevant for your particular situation). So, on the one hand, requiring students to create an account is a good thing.

On the other hand, teaching with extraneous web-based tools that require students to create their own individual accounts and sign in each time it is used can also result in a rocky road for students. Imagine being a student enrolled in four classes, each requiring you to create two accounts for Web 2.0 tools. If all of those tools are unique, that is a total of eight accounts. These eight accounts could easily include three tools that essentially accomplish a similar function.

To ameliorate this type of scenario, it's important to be in dialogue with your colleagues in an effort to understand what other tools are being used–either as individual experiments, small pilots, or department-wide usage–to leverage existing knowledge and resources and, ultimately, collaborate to produce a learning environment that is most effective for students.

SHOWCASE

Pepperdine's Business School has crafted a learning experience for students that packages a variety of Web 2.0 and social media tools that have been adopted across the departments and integrated into the institutional support system. This infrastructure not only allows for a simple one-stop portal for students and faculty to access state-of-the-art learning tools, but its modularity makes for an extremely flexible and dynamic framework where simple but frequent upgrades keep both the instructors and students unflustered and happy.

The environment is referred to as GLEAN (Graziadio Learning Environment and Network) and some of the tools included are: Yammer (a micro blogging tool), Google Apps (email, docs, calendar, text and video chat), Join.Me (screen-sharing with VOIP or phone conferencing via a computer or mobile device), and VoiceThread (for rich, personalized presentations with voice and video). The GLEAN experience is streamlined, providing the Pepperdine student community a thoroughly reviewed, supported, and hand-selected collection of Web 2.0 and and mobile tools woven into their learning.

The driving force behind the existence of GLEAN is student learning. Not only does GLEAN simplify the student experience by ensuring the same tools are used through a students' program completion, it also fosters digital literacy skills, positions graduates for success in our global, mobile society, and increases their capacity to collaborate with their peers at a distance around their busy schedules.

As Susan Gautsch, Director of eLearning and designer of GLEAN at Pepperdine's Business School, shares, "Our students are busy professionals who are learning firsthand how 21st century business works. Having all these tools aggregated and simply interlinked with each other enables them to connect, collaborate, discover, and learn like never before." And students

Figure 2.9 GLEAN logo.

agree. Mary Tabata, a student in Pepperdine's fully-employed MBA program says, "GLEAN has allowed my study group to effectively communicate, share ideas, hash things out in real time or asynchronously, post links for further discussion and collaboratively edit our joint projects. This is so much easier and richer than what we used to do (or pretend we were going to do)."

5. End Product

- If using the tool to author content, what format options are provided for the final product? html embed code, url, export to file (.mov, .mp4, .jpg, .png, etc.).
- If you are producing files, do you have a method of hosting them?

If the tool is being used to author content or share content that is authored outside of the tool, what is the end product? If the product is a file (an image or movie file, for example), you'll need to determine a method for hosting it online and consider any size limitations that may guide your workflow. For example, if you plan to upload video files into a course management system supported at your institution, there is likely a maximum size that has been allotted for your individual use. Knowing this ahead of time is important to ensure you develop an alternative hosting option or request more space if permissible.

Alternatively, if the tool produces a web-based product you should take note of the output options. Does it share a link to your product (http://www. . .), does it provide html embed code (codes vary but typically look like a long string of incomprehensible text like this: <iframe width="560" height="345" src=. . .), or both? Develop a plan for where you will share the link or embedded object (see Chapter 1 for a discussion about the value of embedding vs. linking to online content).

Also, if you are teaching with a course management system, it's a good idea to be sure the version you are using supports the embed code provided by the tool. YouTube's iframe embed code currently causes problems when embedded, for example, in Blackboard 9.1. A workaround is to use the "old embed code" option that YouTube still makes available. A brief conversation with your system administrator is a good idea at this point.

6. Sharing Options

- Do you have options that allow you to restrict access to the content you create (private, unlisted, invitation only, public)?
- If you will be inviting a group of students to use the tool or access the content you've authored, is there an alternative to sending invitations through email (for example, an invitation link)?

Does the tool provide access options for viewing the content? Seek out tools that provide a variety of privacy settings such as:

Private

Viewable by you only, content cannot be viewed by other users and will not be retrieved through a web search.

Those Who Have the Link (Sometimes Referred to as "Unlisted")

Content is viewable by you and any other users who have access to the link, content will not be retrieved through a web search. This option enables embedded content to be viewable in a protected learning environment (like a course management system) but doesn't permit the content to be viewed by the general public. This is a useful sharing option, as the content can be easily shared only with students after they have authenticated as actively enrolled students in your class.

Those Who You Invite

Content is viewable by specific users you have invited. This may require students to "join" (and you to approve their request) and then sign-in before viewing the content. This option should be used with caution, especially if the tool specifies that invites must be sent through email invitations. Spam filters typically "catch" these generic invitations, resulting in confused students who are unable to complete because they never received the invitation you sent. It also results in aggravated professors who find themselves managing lists of students who received and didn't receive the invitation.

Alternatively, many tools provide a process to invite users through "a link" and this works well! The key is to share the link in a place that only your students have access to. Emailing the link directly to your students is one option. And if you have an established email relationship in place, it is unlikely that your email will be devoured by a spam filter. Another option is to place the link inside your course shell in a course management system.

Public

Content is viewable by anyone and will be retrieved through web searches. There are many excellent educational reasons for encouraging 21st-century students to learn in the open web. Doing so fosters digital literacy skills and promotes opportunities for global collaborative projects—skills that are directly relevant to 21st-century success. But don't expect students to *know* they are contributing in an open web environment. It is your responsibility to communicate this to them upfront and, as noted earlier, it's an effective strategy to explain why you've elected a public sharing option for their learning environment. Tips and strategies for managing student privacy effectively in an online environment are included in Chapter 1.

7. Intellectual Property

•   What rights do you have to the work you share through the site?
•   What rights does the site have to sharing your work without your permission?

Social media and Web 2.0 tools will require you to accept a Terms of Service (ToS) prior to your use. If your students are using the tool, they will also be required to accept the terms. Unfortunately, they may be dense and laden with legal jargon that is difficult to comprehend. But it's important for you to understand these terms, particularly the sections that explain how your content may be used and shared without your permission. And be aware that terms of service can change frequently.

Typically, the ToS will cover acceptable behavior and content standards (no objectionable material, pornography, etc.), copyright guidelines (which will stipulate that you take responsibility for ensuring you own the copyright of the content you share and/or have the necessary permissions to distribute copyrighted content), disclaimers that release the site from certain liabilities (for example, the credibility of content shared on the site or responsibility for your content if it is lost in a data failure), a privacy policy (see criteria #8: Privacy), and intellectual property overview.

When examining the intellectual property criteria in a ToS, it's important to remember that online tools are owned by companies seeking to promote their product. Therefore, it's common to see a statement that stipulates: 1) that you (or the copyright owner) maintain the rights to the work you share on the site, 2) that other users must abide by the rights you have defined for your work, and 3) that the site has the right to reproduce your work for however it wishes (usually for marketing purposes).

For example, here is an excerpt from the SlideShare terms of service. SlideShare is an online repository of presentations that conveniently converts PowerPoint or Keynote files into a Flash-based presentation (see Chapter 4 for a further discussion of Slideshare). According to these terms, by using their site you are giving SlideShare permission to use your work and any derivatives of your work in any media format and through any media channel:

> **Nothing in these Terms of Service change, affect or diminish in any way whatever rights Submitters may have in the Submissions.** By submitting the Submissions to SlideShare, however, you hereby grant SlideShare a worldwide, non-exclusive, royalty-free, sublicenseable and transferable license to use, reproduce, distribute, prepare derivative works of, display, and perform the Submissions in connection with the Site and SlideShare's (and its successor's) business, including without limitation for promoting and redistributing part or all of the Site (and derivative works thereof) in any media formats and through any media channels (except to the extent limited by, and expressly stated in the applicable additional terms and conditions for, Premium Services offered by SlideShare).[9]

Here's a story that demonstrates this intellectual property clause in action. I am a SlideShare user. One time, I presented a talk at a conference titled "Teaching in the Age of Participation." This talk was supplemented with a slide-based presentation. Prior to the delivery of my talk, I uploaded the slides to SlideShare and shared the link to the presentation in two ways: 1) in a post on my blog, and 2) in a tweet using the conference hashtag (a simple text sequence, starting with #, that allows for tweets to be indexed and organized into a stream for a group of users to easily follow, read, and reply to in real time).

When an audience member raised her hand and asked if I could share the presentation, I said, "I already have. You'll find it on SlideShare and the link is available on my blog and in the conference's Twitter feed." As the copyright owner of the presentation, I maintained my rights to the content I had uploaded to. If anyone in the audience wanted to redistribute my work or use it in their own work, they would need to abide by my licensing stipulation that I added on the first slide. However, by using SlideShare, I agreed to their Terms of Service, which simultaneously gave SlideShare permission to use my work. That afternoon I received an email notice that my presentation was the most viewed presentation in the "Education" category and was being featured on the SlideShare "Education" page. That's an example of how a company distributes content (often driven by the reviews of other users) to promote and market their site.

In the end, it was just more exposure for my own ideas . . . and I had no problem with that! In fact, it was really fun and exciting to watch my work be tweeted, liked, and "favorited" by so many users. This social media experience, for me, helped validate the relevancy of my ideas and assist me with sharing my approaches, opinions, and perspectives. However, it's often difficult for college professors to feel comfortable with sharing their work. Academic experiences have taught us to protect our ideas and channel them into respected, peer-reviewed publications. This tradition, reinforced by tenure and other traditional incentives, can rub against the grain of the concept of openness and sharing, values that are central to social media.

8. Privacy

- What information is required to create an account?
- How is this information used?
- Is a privacy trustmark displayed?
- Does the tool integrate third party applications?
- How are cookies used?

Let's get this out of the way-social media has redefined the concept of privacy. When you sign up for a new tool, you are asked to provide information about yourself. Don't feel obligated to fill in every field. Rather, just complete the required fields and limit what you share with companies.

The Terms of Service that you agree to before you use a tool clarify how your "personal information" will be used and disclosed. Navigating this information on your own is, unfortunately, tricky and perplexing. I find myself scratching my head each time I dig into a privacy policy.

Trustmarks

Fortunately, more and more sites are finding value in developing more lucid ways to convey their interest in protecting your privacy to the extent possible in the open web. One indicator of trend is the use of "trustmarks" that represent validation by an external privacy service, like TrustE. When you see a TrustE seal on a website you can be assured that the site has demonstrated compliance with TrustE's high standards for protecting the privacy of their users.[10]

Ning, a popular tool (discussed more in Chapter 5) that extends a user the opportunity to create a social network about any topic, displays the TrustE seal within its privacy policy. That's a helpful indication to me, that I am using a site that has taken the time and interest to develop a thoughtful policy.

However, I can't stop there. If I choose to create a Ning network, I will be extended the opportunity to customize my network with add-on applications (like chat, live video streaming, etc.). These applications are enticing and I can add them with a single click. But, by doing so, I am now agreeing to the Terms of Service for those additional applications, which are not as trustworthy as Ning's. In fact, Ning has a separate "Applications Terms of Service" that explains:

> By adding third party applications, you understand and acknowledge that certain information may be shared with or collected by the third party application developer or operator of such application. It is strongly suggested that you consult such third party's terms of user and privacy policy to decide whether you are comfortable with their terms and privacy practices.[11]

As you evaluate tools, look for seals and be aware of these hidden terms that can easily sneak by you!

Ads and Cookies

Sites that are free *may* come along with additional privacy concerns. If a site is free and isn't generating money from a premium service, it's getting paid *somehow* and it's usually through the ads you see permeating the pages. Ads are intrusive to any user's experience because they are simply distracting but they're also intrusive to a user's privacy. It's good to get educated about how those ads work.

Within a site's Terms of Use, you will also see reference to the use of "cookies." A cookie is a piece of text-based information that is transmitting from a site's server and installed on your computer (in your web browser). When you return to a site, it examines your cookies and if it finds familiar information, it will use it to refine what you see on the site. For example, cookies can be used to create customized lists of videos in YouTube based upon your previous viewing patterns or a customized list of books on Amazon. Cookies do not carry viruses but they can reveal personal information about your web activities that may violate your idea of privacy.

Here is an excerpt of YouTube's Privacy Notice explaining how a user's personal information is used:

> We use cookies, web beacons, and log file information to: (a) store information so that you will not have to re-enter it during your visit or the next time you visit YouTube; (b) provide custom, personalized content and information; (c) monitor the effectiveness of our marketing campaigns; (d) monitor aggregate metrics such as total number of visitors and pages viewed; and (e) track your entries, submissions, and status in promotions, sweepstakes, and contests.[12]

So, what's the big deal about cookies? They *are* useful and can customize your experience in a pleasant way but when you're using tools that are proliferated with advertisements, the benefit of cookies can crumble. (Sorry, couldn't resist that one!) For example, WetPaint.com is an entertainment-oriented site that began as a wiki hosting platform. WetPaint wikis are easy to use and customize. But the free version of WetPaint is laden with ads.

When I access a WetPaint wiki, WetPaint sends cookies to my browser. Simultaneously, the advertising company or companies hosting the ads appearing on the wiki page are also sending cookies to my browser. When I log off the site and visit another site with ads, it's possible that the same advertising companies may be hosting those ads. After weeks, months, and years of web browsing, advertising companies collect a lot of information about you and can construct a rich picture of your individual preferences without you even realizing it.

To get more informed about who is tracking your activity as you search the web, Jason Jones recommends an application called Collusion.[13] I was curious so I gave it a try. After installing Collusion, it opens an empty webpage that begins to display sprouting notes as you browse the web. I went to wetpaint.com, which is the portal that extends one access to "WetPaint for Wikis." After opening the site, Collusion revealed that more than nine different companies were tracking my activity from that one site alone.

After reading this section, you may be feeling overwhelmed and trepidatious about the idea of using emerging technologies in your classes. Try to view this information as knowledge that will make you a more informed and effective teacher, as well as a 21st-century citizen. Navigating web pages and joining new online services is part of our life now. Chances are, after finishing this chapter, you'll become much more aware of how frequently you encounter ads online-even when doing something as simple as checking your email. Privacy is one of many threads in the fabric of teaching with emerging technologies and should be considered, along with all the rest of the threads, as you evaluate tools for use, but not act as a roadblock for achieving your goals.

21st-Century Skills

Growing up in a mobile world fosters drastically different perspectives about participation, privacy, credibility, and identity. When my son was 10, he asked me if he could share a video of him with his friends that I had posted to my YouTube account. I said, "Sure, but I shared it as an 'unlisted' video which means they won't find it in a YouTube search so you'll need to send the link to them." He stared at me blankly and asked, "What's the point of sharing a video on YouTube if people can't see it?" To his generation, getting "views" is a sign of worth and social validation. But, unfortunately, he wasn't born with a filter. To understand how, when, and why to share content publicly, he actively participates in sharing videos on YouTube, under the tutelage of his (sometimes nervous) mom. This has allowed him to begin to understand what content is acceptable for the public, what content should be kept public, and what content needs approval or permission from others before it can be shared publicly. By reading and discussing the comments of other users with him, we both are identifying examples of acceptable and unacceptable ethical activities and evaluating the effects of both on a user's credibility.

Our digital information society has transformed the skills that are necessary for living a successful life. Twenty-first-century citizens are expected to be able to search for and evaluate digital information (which now exists in text, image, and video), synthesize ideas, construct opinions, as well as analyze and respond to viewpoints in an ethical way. These skills are fostered most effectively through experiential learning. And this is one of the most important outcomes of teaching with emerging technologies.

Often, the dialogue around 21st-century skills is set within the context of teaching youth. However, higher education is a critical step in achieving new media literacies. Students come to college for a variety of reasons but central to all is an interest in preparing oneself for a successful, meaningful life. The environment—the outcomes, content, activities, and tools used to orchestrate them—plays a critical role in achieving this goal. If students spend their college years passively listening to live lectures in a brick and mortar room, there is little to no opportunity for new media literacies to be acquired. If professors are encouraged, inspired, and incentivized to teach with emerging technologies, the playing field will shift and college will play a formative role in mastering necessary 21st-century skills and encouraging students to develop a credible digital footprint, which will play an important role in an individual's personal and professional success long after college.

Researchers from Harvard, MIT and USC have produced a helpful casebook that contains curricular material for developing "new media literacies." The resource, "Our Space: Being a Responsibile Citizen in the Digital World," (http://www.goodwork project.org/practice/our-space) is shared online with a Creative Commons license, meaning the material is free to use as long as the author is attributed. It is openly available for educators to adopt and integrate into their own curriculum and professional development programs. Resources like this one extend opportunities for lifelong learning to self-motivated college educators but also signal important new curriculum topics for institutionalized professional development programs.

Teaching effectively with emerging technologies requires more than fluency in how to "use a tool." It also requires one to be able to demonstrate how to participate ethically and responsibly in online communities, evaluate the role that online self-expression plays in the formation of one's identity, analyze the opportunities and risks involved with online participation, and assess the credibility of online users and content. This is a complex topic that is vital to the future of higher education and the lives of our students.

Summary

This chapter serves as an important transition for us. It discusses the transition from teaching to learning, drawing from the work of Barr and Tagg, which serves as a framework for this entire book. As you make your journey from delivering content to crafting and facilitating participatory, student-centered learning experiences, you will leverage the tool evaluation criteria included in this chapter. In Chapter 3 you will be provided with a set of "essential" tools to get started and keep moving fluidly through your journey.

Chapter 3

Essentials Toolkit

Tools are like cars. They enable you to move from one point to another. The destinations they take you to is what makes them powerful. In the flipped classroom case study shared in the Introduction, I demonstrated how I leveraged podcasts and VoiceThreads to transform my students' learning. Again, the tools themselves are not important—it's the *experiences* they create that are critical.

The previous chapter provided you with a framework for evaluating tools prior to using them in your class. Chapters 3, 4, and 5 will introduce you to a variety of tools and identify examples of how they can be used. You should keep the evaluation framework in mind as you explore the buffet of tools I will present to you. Some may meet your criteria or spark new ideas for you.

The tools shared in the next three chapters are organized to convey how they can be used to achieve particular goals: to share content; to increase communications with your students; and to create participatory, collaborative learning activities. As you read these next few chapters, you will, undoubtedly, find more uses for them and expand upon the categories I've developed here—that's something to celebrate!

I consider the tools in Chapters 4 and 5 to be "second-tier" tools. They're powerful and important but they work best when added onto an existing "essentials toolkit." The "essentials toolkit" includes a collection of hardware and software that you will use across the spectrum as you engage and participate in emerging technologies. Without these tools, my teaching would crumble.

Disclaimer: technology changes quickly. All descriptions of tools and account characteristics are reflective of services at the time of writing. Please refer to the website of each individual tool for current information.

1. Webcam

 A webcam empowers you to add your social presence to students' learning experiences, even when you are not physically present. You may already have a webcam on your computer—so be sure you check into that before you purchase one.

It can be used to record mini-lecture modules (see "Screencasting" below), personalized announcements (see "YouTube" below), send personalized video emails (see "EyeJot" in the next chapter), and connect with students via synchronous web conferencing and communication tools (Skype, VoiceThread, Google+ Hangouts, etc.).

When shopping for a webcam, I encourage you to peruse the C-Net reviews to identify options that meet your needs. The higher the video output resolution, the better the image quality: http://reviews.cnet.com/webcams/.

TIP

Lighting Matters!

The right lighting conditions will transform the quality of the videos you record with your webcam. Many times users don't think about light and that can result in dark images that render your entire face in silhouette. What's the point of using a webcam if you aren't identifiable? A quick way to ensure you produce quality video with your webcam is to do your recordings with a light source in front of you, rather than behind or to the side of you. When light illuminates the front of your face, you'll be rendered beautifully on camera!

Look at the difference lighting makes in Figure 3.1.

---

2. Microphone

A microphone allows you to communicate online with your voice, which may be more appropriate, at some times, than video. Video conveys your physical appearance, including your gestures and facial expressions, and voice focuses on the qualities of your speech. Also, video files are much bigger than audio files. Think about these elements when deciding which output option is the best for your particular use.

Also, video requires much more preparation than voice. For example, when I use Skype I do not set it to pick up a call automatically with video because I want to be sure my surroundings are appropriate for my audience –and, let's face it, we're not

Figure 3.1 Webcam lighting comparison. Used with permission from VoiceThread.

always ready to present ourselves in video! But I can easily use my microphone and engage directly in a voice-based conversation.

Again, I encourage you to peruse the C-Net reviews at the link below before you make a microphone purchase. I recommend a USB microphone with a headset. This option creates high quality audio recordings and also gives you the option to set your audio output to your headset, allowing you to hear more clearly and filter out background noise: http://reviews.cnet.com/microphones/.

3. Screencasting Software

A screencast is a video recording of your computer's screen. The uses of screencasting in teaching are endless—how-to videos, lectures, an orientation or tour of an online class—they provide quick and effective visual answers to questions, and students can create screencasts to demonstrate their ability to perform online tasks or give presentations.

Not long ago, screencasting tools were expensive and using them required quite a bit of training. In short, just a few years ago screencasting was for experts. Well, not anymore. Today, if you do not already have access to a premium screencasting tool (like Camtasia or Screenflow), there are a number of free to low cost tools that can get you on track for creating your own, customized video content.

Screencast-o-matic—http://www.screencast-o-matic.com

A free, browser-based tool that gives you direct access to creating a screencast with a single click. The application launches a java applet on your computer that runs the screencast. You click "record," resize the cross-hairs to fit the size of your recording, select the microphone option you are using, indicate whether or not you want to also record from your webcam (an added bonus!), click the record icon, wait for the countdown, and go! When you're done, click pause or stop, and then you have the option to upload the video to Screencast-o-matic's server, download it to your own computer (a variety of file options provided) or upload it directly to your YouTube account. The quality of the videos after being uploaded direct to YouTube is impressive. Screencast-o-matic also includes the option to add "call outs" (visual enhancements that draw attention to your mouse clicks and make fine "how-to" details easier to see).

Account Details

Recording is possible with no account. If you create a free account, you'll be able to view and manage your recordings history. A Pro account includes premium features like editing. Videos recorded with a free account will include a small watermark.

Jing—http://www.techsmith.com/jing

If I had to pick one emerging tool that I use the most, it would be Jing. Jing is a tool by TechSmith, the creators of Camtasia and SnagIt, that requires a free download (available for both Mac and PC users) and produces screencasts, as well as screenshots (still image captures of your computer screen). You can set the Jing app to launch each time your computer starts and while it is running, a golden sun icon hovers at the top of your screen.

When you need Jing, you simply activate it with your mouse, click on the 'cross hairs' icon, and drag it across your screen to select the portion you want to capture. When you capture a still image of your screen, you can also annotate on top of the image (call out an area with a colored box, add a line of text, or include an arrow to point out something important). Then you may download the image or video file to your computer *or* upload it directly to your screencast.com account, which is automatically created when you install Jing.

Why is that important? Because in a matter of two minutes, you can create a one-minute video, upload it to the web in a click, and paste a link to the video in an email. And that's what makes Jing so handy. It is irreplaceable when teaching online. I use Jing everyday to answer "how-to" questions from students—and I love hearing their excitement when they realize I sent them a personally recorded video to answer their question. Responding to a frustrated or nervous student with video is a great way to calm their nerves and support them through a class. See Chapter 4 for more about Jing.

Account Details

Jing is free. Jing Pro, a premium service, is no longer available.

4. Online Content Hosting Services(s)

Hosting your content online—"in the cloud"—empowers you to access your content from anywhere, share it easily without emailing large files, and can facilitate virtual collaboration projects. I recommend identifying a video hosting tool and a document hosting tool.

YouTube—http://www.youtube.com Free Online Video Hosting

A free YouTube account provides you with a free hosting resource for video content *you create* and a personal channel that you can use to curate video playlists around focused topics that can be shared with relevant audiences.

- Each video you upload can be set to Public, Unlisted (which means only those who you share the link with can view it), or Private (you identify the individuals who may view it).
- YouTube limits your videos by length (which, at the time of writing, is 15 minutes).
- I use my YouTube account to host video announcements and screencasts (screen recordings) for my classes. This option enables me to customize the privacy setting of the videos and then embed them in my course management system or website I am using for teaching (see Chapter 1 for an overview of linking vs. embedding).

- When you "upload" a video you may select one from your hard drive that you've already created or you can record direct from your webcam (which is what I do for recording online announcements for my students).
- The videos you create can be captioned within a matter of minutes, as long as you have a transcript of your video (saved as a .txt file). For details (and a link to a how-to video) refer to the "Captioning Tool" category below.

TIP

YouTube is more than a video hosting site. I also use it to curate my YouTube content (including the videos I create, as well as the videos I want to save and share with others). My personal YouTube account includes a "channel" on which users can view playlists I have curated. For example, I have one playlist titled, "Teaching with Emerging Technologies," another titled "Daguerreotype and Calotype." As I find videos I want to save, I can add them to a playlist and I can then share each playlist with the related group of users. For example, the "Teaching with Emerging Technologies" playlist is embedded on my blog. The "Daguerreotype and Calotype" playlist is embedded in a unit within my History of Photography class. I also have a playlist titled "History of Photography" where I share mini-lecture-like videos that cover specific topics and themes related to photography.

Each time you share a video on YouTube, you have the option to share it with a Creative Commons license or a traditional YouTube license, providing more opportunities to create a culture of open content and foster lifelong learning around the world.

SHOWCASE

A professor equipped with a webcam, screencasting software, and a YouTube account is a professor who holds the tools to transform online learning from dull and dry to dynamic and personal. I have created a Google Site titled *The Human Touch: Increasing Your Online Presence With Video* which includes tips, strategies, and links to tools to get you started with teaching effectively with video. Visit the site here: http://goo.gl/9LYhc.

Box—http://www.box.com Free Online File Hosting for Fast and Secure Sharing and Collaborating

 A free Box account provides you with an easy way to store documents online and share them with a simple link. Files are secure and can also be shared with specific users to enable collaboration between virtual teams.

- Each document comes along with a public link you can insert into webpages, your course management system and email, as well as embed code which gives you the option to integrate an "image" of your content on a webpage. (If you embed a document, always include the link, as well, because the embedded content is not accessible to students who rely upon screen readers.)

- If you work on a mobile device, use the Box mobile app to access, store, and share your content from anywhere at any time.
- Need to collaborate? Set up a folder and invite select users to have access to its contents. Users can download, edit, upload files and/or leave comments from anywhere with any device.

Account Details

Box has free and an array of premium account options that meet the needs of individual users, as well as large corporations. At the time of writing, a free account provides a user with 5 GB of online storage space and permits individual file uploads up to 25 MB.

Dropbox—https://www.dropbox.com Cloud-Based Storage and Content Back Up

Dropbox is like a mobile Flash drive. It is an application that you install, for free, on your computer. Once installed, a Dropbox icon appears in your toolbar and acts as a separate disk storage location within your everyday workflow. For example, when I go to save a file, I have the choice to save it to my hard drive or my Dropbox folder (functioning the same way a Flash drive would). I can access all the files I save in my Dropbox folder from any device with an internet connection. For example, a computer in my classroom or my iPhone (via the free mobile app). I can also select a folder or group of folders on my hard drive and have them continuously sync to my Dropbox folder, which is a terrific option for a "class presentations" folder, for example.

Account Details

Box has free and premium account options. At the time of writing, a free account provides a user with 2 GB of online storage space. The free account provides secure hosting of content with the inclusion of a "public" folder that enables a process for sharing content with users via a simple link.

TIP

If you have an iPad and use Keynote, download the Dropbox app and use your iPad to present your lectures in class with the Keynote app.

5. A Method for Captioning Videos

As noted above, videos must be captioned to be compliant with federal ADA requirements. When you weave captioning into your workflow, you are establishing a process that makes web accessibility an essential building block in your teaching process. Some faculty are fortunate to have services on their campus that do captioning for them. Many are not and have to do it themselves. Here are a couple of free options.

YouTube: http://www.youtube.com

If you choose to create a free YouTube account and use it to host your own videos, you have a built in captioning feature that is easy to use. The key is to have a text transcript of your video saved in a .txt file. YouTube does not require you to have the timing integrated into your transcript file (which is a huge plus!)

After you record and publish a video, click on the "Edit Subtitles/Captions" tab. Select "Add New Captions or Track," click "Browse" and select your .txt transcript file, select "Transcript File," and then click "Upload file." That's it. In a matter of moments, your captions will be live on your video and they will appear in all embedded versions of the video too.

Here is a link to a 4-minute video illustrating how to add captions in YouTube: http://youtu.be/V3oAR890Cb0.

Wistia: http://wistia.com

If the idea of needing to create a transcript for every video you produce is daunting, Wistia is a service that is definitely worth looking into. Wistia is another video hosting service offering private viewing options, like YouTube, but it provides 100% accurate transcripts within a day or two of uploading your video. And the transcripts are interactive, which means you can search them (imagine being a student who wants to review a particular 2-minute topic covered in a 15-minute video) and click on any word in the transcript and the video will jump to the place in the video in which the word is spoken.

Wistia also provides built-in web analytics for your videos, which they refer to as "real time heat maps." As viewers watch, information they are viewing activity is tracked, allowing you to examine not only how many people have viewed your video but also when each of them stopped viewing it and which pieces were viewed multiple times. The activity is tracked using colors, like a thermal map, and as pieces of the video are watched more than once by a particular viewer, that corresponding segment in the timeline changes from green to yellow and red. This information could be incredibly valuable to instructors or instructional designers to understand what parts of an instructional video are being repeated most frequently by which students.

Account Details

Wistia is not free but you can sign up for a full-service, free trial to evaluate it.

Universal Subtitles: http://www.universalsubtitles.org

While YouTube allows you to add captions to videos *you've* created, you will find times you need to add captions to videos others have created. That's when Universal Subtitles comes in handy. The site is community-oriented and calls upon volunteers to contribute time to caption videos and make them more accessible for more users around the world. You make a request for a video to be captioned, volunteer your time to caption videos, or use the tool to caption a specific online video. After a video is captioned, it becomes available to all users (which means using this tool contributes to a more globally accessible internet community) and may be embedded anywhere.

6. A URL Shortener

While the need for a tool that condenses the length of a URL (link or web address) may not be immediately apparent to you, it will soon enough! Many of the super cool web tools you'll learn about in the following chapters will enable you to create content that is hosted online. Unfortunately, the ease and convenience of these tools comes along with the nuisance of really long URLs. When you share links to your activities, presentations, etc., it may be more effective to shorten them first. And shortened URLs are essential when using microblogging tools that require short posts. Here are a few free options in this category.

bit.ly: http://bitly.com

Includes a helpful bookmarklet which you can download and install in your browser. Once the bookmarklet is installed, a small button is installed in your browser's toolbar. When you are on a webpage and want to shorten its URL, you simply click on the bookmarklet and bam! That's it. You're done. Also provides statistics about your shortened URLs and the option to use customized URLs.

Google URL Shortener: http://goo.gl

Allows you to track your shortened URLs and see how many times each was clicked on. If you use Chrome as your browser, you can embed the bookmarklet into your browser for streamlined URL shortening.

Ow.ly: http://ow.ly/url/shorten-url

This is part of the larger application known as HootSuite, which allows for users to streamline sharing between social networking sites (for example, post to Facebook and Twitter in a single click). But owl.ly can also be used as a standalone URL shortener.

Summary

The toolkit outlined above is like a Swiss army knife for teaching with emerging technologies. If you skip this chapter and move right into the next, you'll be back to this page soon enough! The following chapters will begin to flesh some of the popular ways emerging technologies are being used in higher education and showcase some innovative uses to spark your creative juices. Let's now dive into Chapter 4 and discover some easy strategies for using free to low-cost voice and video tools to add the human touch to your online content!

Chapter 4

Tools for Communication and Content Creation—Beyond Text!

How different would an online learning experience be if a student had the option to see and hear his professor each week? This is a question that Santa Barbara Community College (SBCC) set out to explore in 2010. Douglas Hersh, Dean of Educational Programs and Technology at SBCC, coordinated a study that examined how the integration of a professor's "human presence" into the design of a course would affect online attrition rates. The premise is simple—two groups of students were studied, one group logged into Moodle and was presented with a course that the professor taught using text-based announcements and messaging. The second group of students engaged the same curriculum but were regularly greeted with an embedded 3–5 minute video of their professor at the start of each new learning module and a direct link to Skype for connecting with their instructor in a live voice or video office hour chat.

Referred to as the "Human Presence Learning Environment," the creative course design, illustrated in the image here, packs an array of social tools into the Moodle shell, including Wimba voice boards (like discussion boards in audio), Blackboard Collaborate (synchronous web conference sessions), a feature that communicates which students are online at any given moment, and a "rate your module" block that allows students to rate learning units just like a dinner on Yelp (interestingly, this last feature is only used by about half of faculty who adopt the Human Presence model).

Hersh's research investigates how text-based course interfaces contribute to a feeling of "disconnectedness" and "alienation" within online learners and may contribute to high attrition rates that plague online courses. Perhaps, the SBCC team is on to something. Perhaps emerging technologies hold opportunities for crafting warmer, socialized, and personalized online learning experiences that replicate the human connectedness from the face-to-face classroom. And maybe that sense of relatedness between a student and her instructor is important enough to increase her interest and motivation week after week and contribute to her continued success. After the semester-long study, the SBCC research team found that the student group that engaged the human presence model yielded a 5% higher course completion rate than the other student group and 9.4% increase in academic success. Impressive.

Not long ago, pricey web conference software was the only widely available method for fostering warm, voice and video communications at a distance. Today there are many more options that are free to low-cost, easy to use, and have opened a new doorway to warm asynchronous—or time shifted—conversations and communications.

Figure 4.1 SBCC Human Presence Learning Environment. Used with permission from Dr. Douglas Hersh.

The "Human Presence Model" developed at Santa Barbara City College is an exception not only because it provides validity to the value of using video and voice communication in online learning, but also because it is an example of an institution working to encourage and support faculty to implement a course design that already has these features built in. But even if you are part of an institution that is not yet working at that level of commitment to learning innovations, you too can experiment, evaluate, and share what you've learned with the world.

The tools that are shared in this chapter will extend the opportunity to you to bring your human presence into your online class, as well as create and share presentations and other types of content with ease. Even if these are tools with which you are familiar or have heard of, I'm hopeful that I have contextualized them in an innovative way, opening up new ways of thinking about how technology can be used in the classroom. I have also showcased special features and "add-ons" available for several of these tools, including widgets and buttons that can be inserted into any webpage (or course management system) to increase your students' interactions with you and their peers.

Jing—Visual Communications

 http://www.techsmith.com/jing

Feature Overview

- Free application that requires installation on your computer.
- When you install Jing you simultaneously sign up for a free screencast.com account to which your Jing screencasts (videos) and screenshots (images) are hosted (when you select this option).
- Facilitates seamless creation, hosting, and sharing of screenshots and up to five-minute long screencasts with a simple link.
- Jing is a TechSmith product (creator of SnagIt and Camtasia).

I actually included Jing in the Essentials Toolkit (see Chapter 3) as a screencasting tool but I want to share it here too, in an effort to demonstrate how it can be used in different ways. Jing is a free application that you download and install on your computer (available for both PCs and Macs). Jing, at its simplest, gives you the extra boost to make your online communications visual. Jing saves you time and will infuse your online teaching with clarity, warmth, and personalization.

Scenarios

Here are two scenarios showing how you can use Jing to enhance communication with your students at a distance.

Scenario #1: Responding to Student Questions with Online Video

Robert Kelley, a psychology professor at MiraCosta College, is in his office responding to emails. He receives a notification that a student has made a post in the "Ask a Question" forum he has set up in his online behavioral statistics class. Robert clicks on the link and is taken to the student's post within his course management system. The student's post reads, "Professor Kelley, I am having difficulty understanding the types of errors regarding hypothesis testing. Can you please explain what the difference between them is?"

As Robert prepares to respond to this question, he has two choices. First, he could type his response, taking extra care to explain his ideas carefully and clearly, perhaps using excerpts from the learning module itself to repeat the ideas for reinforcement. Or, in roughly the same amount of time, he could choose to use Jing to create a video reply, enabling the student to both see and hear the response. With Jing and a microphone, Robert can use his computer screen as a whiteboard to answer his student's questions. Not only will he be able to walk his student through a response but he will also infuse his teaching with an encouraging, understanding tone.

He chooses to use Jing and his workflow is simple. To get started he opens up a blank document in skrbl.com (an online collaborative whiteboard application) or MS Paint and uses it as an whiteboard to illustrate the concept to the student. When he's ready to start his demonstration, he moves his cursor and grabs the cross-hair icon from the Jing sun icon hovering in the corner of his screen. He quickly drags the cross-hairs across the portion of his screen he wants to record, clicks the "record video" option, waits for the 3–2-1 countdown, and begins to speak. Making sure his explanation is less than five minutes (the max recording time for Jing), he finishes the recording and clicks "stop." Next he selects from the two upload options presented to him in Jing: upload to Screencast.com or download to his computer. Robert selects the first option and within a few minutes, Jing responds, indicating that the URL to his video has been pasted to his computer's clipboard.

Now Robert returns to the student's question and writes, "That is a great question. I have provided you with a video response to your question. You can view it at http:// . . ." By using Jing, Robert has effectively responded to the student's question in a highly personalized way. The student has not only had his question answered but has had a custom video explanation recorded for him. By listening to his professor's explanation, he feels more connected to the material, the class itself, and has another instructional method available to him to learn the material and meet the course objectives. In addition to this, by sharing the instructional Jing video in the discussion forum, Robert has effectively made it available to all other students who may have the same question.

Scenario #2: Sharing Essay Feedback With Jing

Dan Barnett is a philosophy professor at Butte College. As an online instructor, he is intimately aware of the amount of time it takes an instructor to effectively grade student papers and makes great effort to share constructive feedback with students so they can improve their writing skills but also clearly understand the strengths and weaknesses of their arguments. But Dan wonders if there's a better way to deliver that feedback to his online students. What if he could deliver it with his voice, rather than text on a screen? Could Jing be used to humanize the grading experience for students? And, if so, how would they respond?

So, he tries a new approach in his online Methods of Argument class. After his students submit their paper, he copies all of them into a continuous Word document (inserting a page break between each paper to ensure only one paper is visible on the screen at a time). Then he begins reading and grading the first paper and applies boldface type to the areas of the paper he plans to address in the Jing video. After he has read and graded the paper, he reaches up to the hovering Jing sun, clicks on the cross-hair icon, drags it across the image of the student's paper on his screen, clicks "record video," waits for the 3–2–1 countdown and speaks directly to the student, using the boldface type to guide him.

When he's done, he clicks "stop" and then opts to upload the video to Screencast.com. Jing promptly produces a unique URL for the video, copies it to his computer's clipboard, and Dan pastes the link into the feedback area for the assignment within the secure gradebook of his course management system. He continues this process until all the papers are graded.

Cynthia, one of Dan's students, logs into the course management system, notices that her grades have been updated and accesses her gradebook information. In the "paper" column, she views her letter grade and sees the link to the video in the "feedback" area. She clicks on the link and views the 5-minute video. While her professor's feedback suggests improvements, hearing his voice adds a human element to her experience. She really understands where he is coming from, how she could improve her writing and doesn't have hurt feelings like she often has after viewing a grade online in conjunction with written feedback.

After conducting a survey with his students, Barnett learned that about 70% of the students viewed the video feedback he shared and three students viewed their video twice. One student shared:

> [The] tone of [your] voice and body language are very important so even if something comes across as sounding a bit harsh, hearing it in your mannerism and soothing voice, softens the words and it sounds gentle and encouraging. I am an extremely sensitive person and I get my feelings hurt easily. I love to write and have done very well in other writing classes but have found this class very difficult, so any criticism is difficult for me, even though I know I need it to succeed.

The data and open-ended student comments are valuable to Barnett, as they help him evaluate whether or not his innovative approach to grading is helpful to students. He shares with me, however, that the students who need the most help are the least likely to view the videos which is a reminder that emerging technologies are, by no means, magical.

Finally, it's a good idea to check with your institution regarding student privacy policies before delivering student feedback via a link generated through a third-party tool (even without a grade). These policies can vary greatly from college to college.

EyeJot—Video Email

 http://www.eyejot.com

Feature Overview

- Free and premium accounts.
- Record video email messages up to 5-minutes in length with a free account.
- Videos can also be embedded in a webpage or course management system.
- All accounts include an embeddable EyeJot widget that creates a simple video communication portal for you and your students within a website or course management system.
- Mobile support—Premium accounts include a mobile-supported inbox. Free account holders may purchase a mobile app.

Arguably, email is the most used technology in college teaching. And, for that reason, EyeJot is a tool that many professors have welcomed into their toolkits. Sending an EyeJot is very similar to using a web-based email client—you compose the message, address it by entering the recipient's email address or sending it to a group you've created, and click "send." The user on the other end receives a notification in their email inbox that they've received a new EyeJot message. The recipient clicks on it and instead of reading a text-based email message, they see and hear you in video! Yes, it really is that simple. And all it requires is a webcam and a free EyeJot account.

My favorite part of EyeJot is that the recipient does not need an EyeJot account to view the message, and they are viewable through any web browser. Some mobile devices still create a hiccup, however, because EyeJot is Flash-based, but premium accounts offer mobile support and there is an iPhone app that may be purchased for $3.99.

Interestingly, I was first introduced to EyeJot by one of my online students. Soon after the start of the semester, a student named "Melanie" sent me an EyeJot in which she asked a question and shared with me that she is dyslexic. She mentioned that she prefers using EyeJot to communicate because it allows her a method of expressing herself without the challenges that reading and writing brings for a person with dyslexia.

Melanie taught me a lot and her honest and personal EyeJot message encouraged me to see new reasons to explore the use of emerging technologies in my teaching. Melanie continues to play an important role in my teaching today, as I now consciously seek out ways to integrate video communications into my classes to create a more inclusive environment in which all students are empowered to learn and communicate in methods that meet their own unique needs.

As for teaching with EyeJot, I like to keep it in my back pocket and use it for instances when I feel like a student needs an extra boost of encouragement. There's really something special to a student about getting a motivational email message from her professor. Try it—make a student's day!

Andrea Neptune, an English professor at Sierra College, began using EyeJot for a very different reason. Soon after beginning to teach online, she developed a painful case of carpel tunnel syndrome induced by grading multiple sets of papers crunched into a several-day period. In an effort to reduce her pain, scale back on her medication, and get rid of her new arm brace, Neptune began experimenting with EyeJot to send video feedback to her students in response to their paper submissions.

Neptune admits, "While the cause of my using EyeJot is not so glamorous, the results have been outstanding." She explains her simple workflow:

> After reading each paper, I highlight areas on screen that I want to comment on, whether positive or negative. I then access the EyeJot website and begin recording. With the document open on screen and its highlights in front of me, I talk my way through the paper, usually noting the paper's strengths and weaknesses as well as making suggestions for revision. I then send the video via email to each student, and students can access the videos without needing to download software or paying a fee.

Neptune adds, "EyeJot is especially effective in my creative writing courses as I can comment on the theme, setting or characters in their stories globally without needing to refer to minute grammatical details. Students can also watch the video repeatedly as they revise their papers."

EyeJot has been such a great resource for Neptune that she has begun to use it for more than just feedback. She also uses the tool to send out an introductory greeting to her online classes the first week of the semester so they can, as she explains, "see my face and listen as I explain the course format, making them realize there is a 'human' at the other side of the screen." Neptune also uses the "embed" feature of EyeJot to insert video reminders, assignment explanations, and a farewell end-of-the-semester wrap-up message into her courses. She notes, "I have even had students reply to me using their own Eyejot videos, which is wonderful! Students have told me they have felt more engaged in my classes because of the personal connection, and that makes all the difference.

As a friendly reminder, email is not a secure method for communicating grades to students. While EyeJot can be a terrific tool for sending personalized, warm feedback to your students, be sure to use a secure environment, like a course management system, for communicating grades. When in doubt, it's always best to check with your institution to ensure your practices are in compliance with your local student privacy guidelines and policies.

TIP

Create a Video Communication Portal With the EyeJot Widget!

Each EyeJot account includes a feature referred to as an EyeJot widget. A "widget" is a miniaturized version of an application that can be installed on a website by copying and pasting a string of html code into the source code view of a webpage. The EyeJot widget allows you to post a brief video message on a website that stays there and serves as a video communication portal for users. Students can click on and send you a video message from their own free Eyejot account.

Figure 4.2 EyeJot widget. Used with permission from EyeJot.

In a course I teach with Moodle, I embed an EyeJot widget that I've titled "Send Michelle an EyeJot!" on the course's homepage (doing this is trickier in some other course management systems like Blackboard which prevent you from integrating html blocks into the top layer of your course). When a student clicks "Reply," he is given an opportunity to compose and send a video message directly from the widget! In other words, the player that plays my recorded message transforms into a camera and records the EyeJot without requiring the student to leave the course page. The EyeJot message sent by the student appears in my inbox along with all of my other emails.

The widget is a great way to foster more personalized connection with your students. I have found that the quality of the messages I receive via video are very different from written emails also. Students are, in general, more willing to share challenges, reflections, and concerns with me when they're given a simple, private method of communicating at a distance with video. It really does shift the playing field (in a good way).

Skype—Synchronous Voice, Video, and Text

http://www.skype.com

Feature Overview

- Free and premium account options.
- Requires software to be downloaded (supports both PC and Mac).
- Free mobile app available.
- Helpful status buttons keep students informed about your current availability.

Skype is widely used in education and I may be taking a risk here by identifying it as "emerging" but I still encounter so many instructors (and students) who think it's a premium service that it's worth sharing. Skype is available for free, works great on both PCs and Macs and offers mobile apps to support most devices. I've never paid a dime for Skype and I use it widely to communicate synchronously with students via voice, video, and text; as well as for work (scheduled interviews for this book, impromptu meetings with colleagues, and fabulous video interactions with relatives who I don't see enough). And the Skype mobile apps are quite fantastic, allowing you to be accessible via Skype from anywhere at any time. This is a nice option for connecting with students, as it provides you and them with a free method of connecting without sharing your mobile phone number.

After downloading Skype, you can start searching for contacts and adding them to your contact list. Each user can opt to be contacted directly by another Skype user or can require users to request permission to add them to their contact list. Once you have a contact in your list, simply click on their name and then select from typing an instant text message or making a voice or video call. It's that simple. Additional features in the free service include conference voice calls between groups of up to 25 Skype users and one-to-one screensharing, which is a lovely feature for tutoring an individual student in an online office hour setting.

Recording Calls

Also check out the many options for third-party call recorders that are available for Skype. This is something you will likely have to pay for but it really starts to expand the options for using Skype. Think about using a call recording add-on to create an archive of audio or video interviews with experts from your field that you can have students access for future projects—or have students add their own interview recording for a creative twist to a traditional research project. There are many options here and more are surfacing all the time so do some searching on your own. Here are a couple options:

- **Pamela Call Recorder:**
  - http://www.pamela.biz/
  - PC only, free (records up to a 15-minute audio call and a 5-minute video call).
- **IMCapture for Skype:**
  - http://www.imcapture.com/IMCapture-for-Skype/
  - Mac and PC, premium service with free trial. Records audio and video calls.

TIP

Use a Skype Status Button to Keep Your Students Informed About Your Availability

Skype buttons (similar to widgets) can be used to make you more accessible to your students. I use one in a course I teach with Moodle. By adding a simple HTML Block to my Moodle course page, I can easily paste the html code for the button into the box and the button magically appears (be sure to click the HTML Source icon in the toolbar first. Also see the "Embedding" section in Chapter 1 for help). The button can be installed on any webpage that accepts html code.

To customize the html code for my button, I first go to "Get a Skype button" page at: http://www.skype.com/intl/en-us/tell-a-friend/get-a-skype-button/. Then I select the button I want, in this case the "status button," and enter my Skype username into the appropriate box.

Figure 4.3 Skype status buttons. Used with permission from Skype.

Copy & paste this code

Show ⦿ Web HTML ◯ Email HTML

```
/js/skypeCheck.js">
</script>
<a href="skype:mpacansky-
brock?call"><img
src="http://mystatus.skype
.com/balloon/mpacansky-
brock" style="border:
none;" width="150"
height="60" alt="My
status" /></a>
```

Figure 4.4 Skype embed codes. Used with permission from Skype.

The html code is automatically customized with my Skype username. Then I copy the code from the "embed code" box, go to my Moodle course page, add an HTML Block to the page, click on the "View HTML Source" icon in the tool bar (looks like this < >) and click "save." That's it!

The button is now embedded on my course page and since the code is linked to my Skype account, it will display a real-time status message to my students, letting them know when I'm online (which means I'm accepting calls), offline (signed out), or can't talk (my status is set to "do not disturb"), or when I'm away (which means I'm still online but have stepped away from my computer). The button is very helpful to me, as it enables me to designate when it's appropriate for students to contact me and keeps my presence very visible each time my students log into the class.

SHOWCASE

Skype Opens Gateway for International Guest Speakers

Lori Rusch is a vibrant art history professor who teaches at multiple institutions throughout the Los Angeles area—including Rio Hondo College, Cal State LA and has also taught advanced level art history courses at Los Angeles County High School for the Arts. The story I am about to share here is one of the most inspirational stories I've heard about using technology in the classroom to empower student learning.

Rusch is a self-proclaimed "Freeway Flyer," a term used frequently in California to describe the reality of part-time instructors who teach at multiple campuses (often with no office but their car trunks and limited access to campus resources), usually with little certainty about the existence of their job from term to term. I share this context because I think it's important to relate to the complexities and challenges that many faculty members navigate continuously while trying to meet the needs of their students. Despite these circumstances, Lori's commitment and passion to teaching and innovation in the classroom shines.

The event from her high school class that is shared here was not part of Lori's plan for her course—it was a spontaneous move to respond to an unexpected interest and enthusiasm that had bubbled up to the surface in her class as her students were shown excerpts of Nigel Spivey's video series, "How Art Made the World." *Who* would ever imagine that an art historian could become a celebrity on a high school campus? Go figure. Rusch allowed her students' energy, curiosity, and wonder to flow naturally until one day, while listening to students enthusiastically mimic Spivey's English accent, she suggested, "Well, why don't you contact him and see if he'd chat with us?"

The students were stunned. Surely, Spivey was "untouchable" to high school students. He is, after all, a celebrity. They even asked, "Why would *he* want to talk to *us*?" Rusch contextualized things a bit and explained that Dr. Spivey is a real person and a real professor—a teacher—at Cambridge University and if he is an educator, why would he *not* want to speak to a group of students? With conviction a student asked, "Do you think we could do a video conference with him?" And that's how it all began.

In the coming weeks, the students worked together (again, remember *none of this* was for credit) to draft a letter to Dr. Spivey which their teacher sent to him on their behalf at his Cambridge email address. Not long after, he accepted their invitation. Rusch suggested to him that the conversation be facilitated with Skype and the two of them connected one time in advance to be sure the technology would be capable of managing an overseas video exchange (both users were utilizing the free version of Skype).

Meanwhile, to help accommodate the students' desire to work as a team to develop interview questions, Rusch elected to set up a Facebook page for the students who had accounts to use (most were already using the service). The students interacted between class meetings to collaboratively draft the interview questions for Spivey's virtual visit to their class. As the date grew closer, they also created posters for the event and began to hang them around campus.

The interview occurred on a Friday morning—two hours before the students' classes actually began. Colleagues shook their heads at the antics. One told Lori that she'd be lucky to "get two kids to show up." They were wrong, oh so wrong! Not only did students come, they packed the room. These students arrived to hear/see this interview because they were excited and inspired, *not because they had to be there*. All the myths and comments I've heard about students "these days" being apathetic and unwilling to do more than they're required to do are capsized by this story—which, I think, is why I love it so much! And it crystallizes the difference a great teacher can make; one who is committed to being flexible to support, guide and cultivate the fluidity of her students' energy through the process of learning.

The interview went without a hitch, except for a two-second delay before Spivey's video image appeared. The students, one after another (a few dressed in outfits that mirrored the attire that Spivey wore in his video series), approached the webcam and asked Spivey the questions they had prepared while the rest of the students watched and listened.

If you'd like to watch a partial video recording Rusch made of the interview as well as a presentation she created and shared on SlideShare, visit the Chapter 4 resources shared online at: http://www.teachingwithemergingtech.com.

═══════════════════

Prezi—an Interactive, Presentation Canvas

 http://prezi.com/

Feature Overview

- Free and premium accounts available.
- The free educator account includes the option to make your content private and customize it with your own logo.

- An iPad viewer is available but creating Prezis on mobile devices is not currently an option.
- May be downloaded for offline viewing.
- May be shared with a link or embedded on a website/course management system.

Chances are you already have a presentation tool in your toolkit—and it's probably Powerpoint or maybe Keynote. Well, Prezi redefines the presentation playing field by transforming your canvas from a sequential, linear sequence of slides to a flat canvas that zooms in and out. When you start a new Prezi, it's much like standing in front of a huge, blank wall on which you have the freedom to group your topics in clusters and plug-in images, links to websites, videos, or voice messages to tell your story. The nature of the Prezi interface will likely compel you to integrate more rich media rather than fall back on the age-old text on a slide. For this reason, it's a compellingly different tool and it shouldn't be theorized simply as a replacement for a presentation tool.

If you use Prezi to create a presentation that you plan to deliver to a group of students, it's a good idea to download it first and use the off-line Prezi viewer to show it (or at least do so as a back up). This way, you aren't dependent upon a network connection for an effective presentation. Aside from using it as a presentation tool, however, Prezi is also an attractive option for creating online learning modules. Simply share the link with your students and they can manually click through the content and watch as Prezi zooms in and out on the content you've added. When students are presented with a video, they may watch it. When presented with a link to a webpage, they may open it.

On the flip side, it's important to think about all your students when teaching with Prezi. First, focus your content when using Prezi and be gentle with the motions you incorporate into the viewing experience. Too much zooming in and out and circling around can result in a disorienting experience for students (particularly those with cognitive disorders) and will, ultimately, detract from your message. Also, if you include a lot of hyperlinks, it's important to make it clear which links they're expected to review and what, specifically, you expect them to do once on that site. Remember to direct their focus and keep the content tied to your learning objectives. Finally, Prezi is Flash-based which, currently, is not accessible to students who rely upon screen readers to navigate online content.

Another option for integrating Prezi is to offer it as an option for your students to use if you regularly require them to create presentations. Some students may find the unique interface a refreshing change from Powerpoint.

==========

TIP

Use Prezi Meeting for Student Collaborations

Each Prezi has the potential to become collaborative with a feature called "Prezi Meeting." Use this feature to invite up to 10 users to collaborate on your Prezi in a synchronous or asynchronous manner. This is an intriguing feature that could foster some very exciting small-group classroom collaborations. Imagine giving students 30 minutes to create a compelling advertisement in support of (or against) a politician. This collaborative activity assumes that students will either have their own laptop or have access to a classroom computer. One alternative approach to support more students would be to have a minimum number of computers in each group.

Animoto—Sleek, Hip Videos Created From Images, Text, Video, and Audio

 http://animoto.com

Feature Overview

- Easy-to-use, online or mobile video creation tool.
- Free and premium account options.
- Free accounts include free 30-second videos.
- Free mobile app for iPhone, iPod Touch, and iPad supports video creation.
- Videos may be shared with a link, embedded on a website or course management system, uploaded directly to YouTube, or downloaded to your computer.
- Create videos from still images, video clips, and pre-recorded audio files.
- A library of royalty-free images and songs are provided at no cost.

Animoto is a super, easy-to-use web-based tool that will make you look like a video editing pro! Once you create your first Animoto video, you'll quickly see the influence of the company's co-founder and ex-MTV producer, Jason Hsiao. And then, after you've created several videos of your family and friends (which you *will do* because it's that fun!), you'll start to see the possibilities Animoto opens for your classes.

Animoto has a simple, step-by-step interface that walks you through creating a video using images, video, and audio files saved to your computer; retrieved from the Animoto media library; or from your Facebook, Flickr, Picasa, Photobucket, and SmugMug accounts. You can easily reorder the media in the creation canvas and add blank slides to which you add your own text. Then select the music for your video from Animoto's royalty-free library, organized by genre with lots to choose from, or your own .mp3 file (be careful about copyright violation here and keep the criteria for Fair Use in mind if you apply copyrighted music to your work, see Chapter 1).

Then sit back and relax while Animoto mixes a super, hip masterpiece for you! When your video is done, you'll receive an email with a link. The video, now hosted at Animoto.com, can be shared to Facebook, YouTube, embedded on a website or in a course management system, and you have the option to download a high-res, DVD-quality copy for a nominal fee.

I have used Animoto to create lively video "bumpers" for my classes. I enjoy sharing them with my students for a high-energy start to the semester. You may view one example here: http://youtu.be/mA1IALdP-tY.

I have also used Animoto to recognize and award significant student achievement. During a semester-long blogging project, I invite students to nominate two peers who have demonstrated "blogging excellence" throughout the semester. I secretly collect the nominations and announce the winner(s) who are rewarded with extra credit points. I have used Animoto to mix in screenshots from the student blogs and showcase the work of the award recipients in a special video presentation. View the video here: http://youtu.be/-N27AFQKYDE.

Anna Stirling, a faculty member at Mt. San Jacinto College, has her students create 30-second Animoto videos in her Introduction to Microsoft Excel class. After a three-week module, the students were instructed to create a "promo" video of Excel to market it to other students. The students were challenged to visually communicate the most important features of Excel using screenshots, as well as images, to symbolically represent their messages. The students posted a link to their videos in a discussion forum and engaged in a dialogue about each others' solution to the problem.

TIP

Get an Educator Account for Free Videos!

Sign up for an educator account at: animoto.com/education, and receive a free Plus account for six months. Includes unlimited creation of full-length videos for you and 50 of your students!

VoiceThread—Multisensory, Asynchronous Conversations Around Media

 http://www.voicethread.com

Feature Overview

- Web-based tool, no downloads.
- Facilitates conversations in voice, video or text around your own curated media collections (images, presentations, videos, documents, and more).
- Free and premium account options, as well as department and site licenses.
- "Doodle" feature provides ability for users to annotate on a slide while commenting.
- Voice comments can be made with a microphone or your own telephone.
- Additional media "slides" can be added at any point.
- Easy "copy" feature streamlines the reuse of content from one term to the next.
- VoiceThreads may be exported into a portable movie file shared with a link, or embedded on a webpage.
- A free mobile app provides access to all your VoiceThreads, as well as the ability to create and/or comment.

- Privacy options range from fully secure, to semi-private, to public.
- Groups feature provides an easy way to manage and share VoiceThreads with different classes.
- Add online images directly from Flickr, Facebook, or the New York Public Library.

VoiceThread provides an easy and free method of uploading a presentation to the web and turning it into a multisensory conversation between you and your students. A VoiceThread can contain a single slide or 500 slides, allowing you the flexibility to use it for straightforward communications with students, interactive tutorials, or diverse learning modules comprised of a mix of videos, presentation slides, images and more. The possibilities are endless, really.

What's especially nice about VoiceThread are the choices it extends to students. If you enable the "commenting" feature in a VoiceThread (which is how you transform it from a linear presentation to an interactive one), students can leave a comment after they have created and logged into their free account. Each student chooses their preferred method: text, voice, or video (or a combination of all three).

VoiceThread could be used in an online class to introduce a new project or your course syllabus. For example, imagine yourself in a classroom with your students. When you distribute a document for a project to them, you wouldn't pass it out and simply tell them to read it. Rather, you would stress key areas of the document, point out important dates and grading criteria, and perhaps summarize some tips and advice for students. Similarly, you do the same thing with a new course syllabus at the start of the term. With VoiceThread, you would simply log into your account, click the "Create" tab, click "Upload" and browse for your document on your computer, and watch as VoiceThread translates the pages of your file into "thumbnail" views. At that point, you could click and drag the thumbnails to reorder them or add a brief video introduction by clicking "Upload from webcam." Then you move onto the "comment" step. Simply click the arrow to move to the slide on which you want to comment, then click the comment button and select from voice, video, or text. Each time a user leaves a comment on a slide, his or her profile picture appears along the edge. The method of commenting is not apparent until a comment is played.

By selecting the video comment option, you could create a personalized intro-duction to a new project or overview of your course syllabus. Additionally, as you comment, you have the option to use your mouse (or finger, if you're using the free mobile app) to annotate directly on your slide with the "doodle" tool. When students play your comments, they will see your doodles in sync with your video comment so it's easy to circle an area of the text while you're discussing it.

If you enable the commenting feature in your VoiceThread, students will see the "comment" button at the bottom of the screen and be able to ask questions about the project—and even circle parts of the document that they're unclear about.

There are many account options available for VoiceThread. Free accounts provide unlimited text and voice comments (with a microphone) and up to 30 minutes of webcam commenting. However, only three minutes of phone commenting is included in a free account (one hour may be purchased for $10). If you plan to *require* students to leave comments in voice or video, it is important to note the expectation of having access to a microphone or webcam in your syllabus. VoiceThread Department and Site Licenses provide the ability to customize the features within your account, allowing you to purchase a bulk of phone commenting minutes that can be distributed to students who do not have another method of leaving a voice or video comment.

TIP

Create Movies and Podcast Episodes With VoiceThread's "Export" Feature

Few VoiceThread users take full advantage of the robust possibilities of VoiceThread. The "export" feature transforms any VoiceThread into a mobile .mov file that can be uploaded to YouTube, played on a mobile device, and is formatted appropriately for iTunes U (if your institution uses this free service from Apple).

TIP

VoiceThread Universal Supports Students Who Use Screen Readers

Sometimes colleges and universities don't consider using VoiceThread because of the fact that it is Flash-based and, as noted earlier, content wrapped in a Flash player does not support screen readers, an accessible technology device used by students who are blind. Fortunately, VoiceThread has a slick "back door" option referred to as VoiceThread Universal that you can point your students to if they need it. Students who use VoiceThread Universal have access to the same content within an html interface that can be navigated with a full screen reader. At the time of writing, it is still in beta and only accommodates text comments from users. Explore VoiceThread Universal at http://voicethread.com/universal/.

TIP

Save Time With the VoiceThread for Moodle

Institutions that use Moodle should consider a department- or site-wide integration of VoiceThread to make use of the time-saving custom integration features VoiceThread has developed for Moodle. For example, the "Authentication" module allows for students to create VoiceThread accounts with a single click, the "Assignment" module saves time by allowing faculty to add VoiceThread assignments from within a course that create a link from the Moodle gradebook to the VoiceThread. The module alleviates the need to fuss with embed code by displaying a visual collection of the instructor's VoiceThreads and embedding any of them with a single click.

SlideShare—Social Online Presentations With Interactive Text

 http://www.slideshare.net

Feature Overview

- Free online hosting of presentations (Powerpoint, Open Office, and Keynote) and documents (PDF and varieties of MS Office, Open Office, and Apple iWork Pages).
- Content may be shared with a link or embedded in a website/course management system.
- Free accounts provide the option to allow users to download your presentations and provide a range of privacy settings for you to opt in or out of the social network component of SlideShare.
- Easily integrate any video on YouTube into your presentations.
- Upload links to your pre-recorded audio files to create a "Slidecast."
- Content can be edited, replaced or deleted at any time.
- A premium account includes many added features, including: private sharing, detailed analytics, a customized channel (or homepage), and the option to upload videos too.
- Mobile Notes: In September 2011, SlideShare shifted from using Flash to html 5. Content uploaded after this change is viewable on iPhones, iPod Touches and iPads. There are plans in place to migrate older content as well.

Powerpoint is a fixture in the higher ed teaching landscape which makes SlideShare a functional and helpful tool for migrating into emerging technology landscape. As you upload presentations to SlideShare, you begin curating your own collection of presentations (which are fully public if you have a free account). SlideShare is more than a site to upload content to, however; it is also a social network. Much like Facebook and LinkedIn, you can "follow" other users, which creates an interesting way to connect with others in your area of expertise.

Once you've uploaded a presentation with a free account, you are given the option to designate whether or not others may download your presentations and can choose to license your work with a traditional "all rights reserved" copyright license or choose from a variety of Creative Commons copyright licenses (see Chapter 1 for more information about Creative Commons licenses). SlideShare automatically translates all the text from your presentation into a simple html transcript that appears below your media. This is a helpful feature for students, as it makes your presentations searchable by text and also provides a more readable version for students who rely upon screen readers.

Also, there is a method for adding audio to your SlideShare presentations, resulting in what is referred to as a Slidecast, but it's a bit involved and requires some knowledge of audio recording, as well as a method for hosting your audio files. Essentially, by "editing" any of your existing SlideShare items, click on the "Create Slidecast" option. Then either upload an .mp3 (audio file) from your computer or link to one that is already hosted online. SlideShare will divide your audio file into segments, based upon the number of slides in your presentation. The audio is synced to the slides based upon this sequence, which means, if you want your audio to play along with your slides, as it would in a "real" presentation, you will need to spend some time using the synchronization tool in SlideShare. It's not difficult to use but it does take time. Also, this process assumes that you have working knowledge of audio recording software. Audacity (http://audacity.sourceforge.net) is a good, free, open-source audio recording software that would be a good fit for recording .mp3 files to import into SlideShare.

If you use SlideShare in support of your teaching, you have the option to upload presentations and embed them on a website or in your course management system for your students, and provide them the option to download them, if you prefer. This workflow may provide more flexibility to part-time instructors who teach at multiple institutions—allowing you to have a centralized location for storing your presentations. For example, if you have a presentation that you share with three different classes that you teach at two separate institutions that each use a different course management system (a tough reality for many part-time instructors!), you would need to replace each of those individual presentations each time you revise the master version. Alternatively, if you were to upload that presentation to SlideShare and embed it in the three separate classes, you can easily replace the version shared on SlideShare and the updates are automatically visible via the embedded versions. Remember, embedded content simply refers back to the server on which the content is housed and it can be a helpful strategy in simplifying your workflow.

I use SlideShare when I present at conferences and workshops. I upload my presentation before I speak and either share the URL with the audience or embed the SlideShare version in a new blog post and point the audience to my blog to retrieve it. This is a huge time saver for me and prevents the need to collect email addresses from those who wish to have a copy of the presentation. I've also met dozens of people online through SlideShare that have learned from the ideas in presentations.

Smashwords—Create Your Own eBook From a Regular Document

 http://www.smashwords.com

Feature Overview

- Free, online service.
- Create and distribute your own eBooks from a Microsoft Word document.
- Smashwords distributes your work to a wide range of major eBook resellers.
- Offer your book for free or set a price.

eBooks are growing in popularity across the college student demographic—and they're becoming more popular with professors too. While not all of us are ready to give up our paper books (and many never will be), it's helpful to know about an easy way to produce and publish your own eBooks using Microsoft Word and Smashwords.

eBooks are a fabulous option for sharing information you have written with your students (perhaps, a course pack, how-to guides, study sets, etc.) but they move beyond the possibility of a printed book because they create a digital canvas in which you may include hyperlinks to videos or other sites to help illustrate your ideas.

Provided you are the original author of a written work, you can create a free account at Smashwords and upload your MS Word document (following the "Smashwords Style Guide") and Smashwords will translate it into the eBook format you specify *and distribute it* to a variety of major eBook distributors, including the Apple iPad Bookstore, Barnes & Noble, Sony and Kobo. Your book is also automatically promoted on Smashwords' own site and an ISBN will be produced for each of your works—at no cost to you.

There is no set-up fee and you have the flexibility to upload updates to your book at any time. Authors select the type of formats in which they want their work to be shared and options include html (for online reading), Kindle, ePub (Apple iPad, Nook, Sony Reader, and more), PVB (Palm Viewing Devices) and more traditional formats like PDF and RTF.

When you publish your work via Smashwords, you have the option to make it available to the public at no cost or for a price determined by you. If you've earned more than $1,000 on Smashwords, you can apply to have your book be distributed via Amazon.

Summary

This chapter has provided you with a collection of emerging tools that can be used to enhance your communications and the sharing of content with your students. The set of tools discussed in this chapter by no means includes all of your options, but such tools are offered to inspire you to see the possibilities of moving your online communications and content beyond the realm of text. Audio, video, images, and mobile devices are the 21st-century palette from which you are invited to craft your own masterful learning experience. When students sit in front of a computer to learn, they will be more engaged and motivated week after week in a long semester journey when they can see you, hear you, and have options to learn from anywhere.

In the next chapter, you will explore more tools that open up an array of possibilities for participatory learning and student-generated content, the next step in transforming your teaching through emerging technologies.

Chapter 5

Backchannels and Tools for Participatory Learning

Twitter? Really?

At one time, I resisted the idea of using Twitter—with passion. I was already feeling over-committed to the number of social networks I had joined and was feeling excited about many new tools I was using. For the life of me, I could not justify why I would want to use a tool that was going to spit out up to 140-character message updates about what people are doing. Really? Me a "tweeter"? What was I going to do? Follow Justin Timberlake? I had written Twitter off as an annoying, immature, superficial nuisance that clearly would add no value to my existence.

Then I found myself sitting at a conference with the complex, multi-colored session brochure laid out in front of me. I was intensely analyzing the sessions, narrowing them down by circling the ones I thought looked best—always finding more than one at each time that I wanted to go to. As I was doing this, the presenter of the general session was informing participants about the Twitter "hashtag" for the conference. I felt stupid because, while I had heard of Twitter, I had no clue what on earth a "hashtag" was and she didn't clarify. I guess that was the moment I felt, one, like I was being left behind (a feeling I don't like much when it comes to new technologies) but also a little intrigued. Here I was at a conference for higher education focused on emerging technologies and Twitter was integrated front and center. I could feel myself trying to avoid it but deep down I knew I was going to have to give Twitter a try.

Reluctantly, I set up my Twitter account and made my first Tweet, revealing my aversion, "Here it goes—another social networking tool. Could it be time for therapy?" Like most "social" technologies, Twitter didn't feel social immediately. The early stages of using a new tool involves the cultivation of your community which includes the users you want to follow and those who follow you. That part took awhile.

So, I set out to decode the "hashtag" concept that had been referenced earlier in the day. I was on to something when I noticed that while I was sending my Tweets from my account on Twitter.com, there was a neat little stream of Tweets appearing in a live feed on the conference website—packaged nicely into a little vertical box. Each of those messages included the hashtag for the conference. A hashtag is, simply, a word or group of characters preceded by the hash (or number) sign, #. Hashtags allow users to tag their Tweets with words or phrases that allow other users to locate, collect and follow real-time conversations about specific topics. Hashtags, essentially, allow anyone to use Twitter for real-time chats, providing an easy method for filtering out the "noise" you don't care about and honing in on messages that have been labeled by users with the same hashtag you are using. This is why it makes sense for a conference or a class to identify a hashtag and instruct participants to use it.

The neat little packaged feed of Tweets I saw on the conference website is referred to as a "search widget" (we explored widgets in Chapter 4 in our discussion of EyeJot). Again, a widget is like a miniaturized and sometimes customized version of an application that can be embedded on a website or in a course management system (see Chapter 1 for details on embedding).

Twitter offers several types of widgets in the site's "resources" area (http://twitter.com/about/resources): a "profile" widget that shares your most recent Tweets, a "search" widget that locates and displays Tweets with the keyword or hashtag of your choice, a "faves" widget that displays Tweets you have marked as your favorites, and a "list" widget that provides a method for organizing Tweets sent by users you have curated into groups or, as Twitter calls them, "lists."

Grasping the widget element of using Twitter was a big step in understanding how a user, like me, could locate, extract, and organize information relevant to my needs from the messy, matted, and unappealing ball of hair that I imagined Twitter to be. Now I was beginning to see the relevance of this pesky little tool and understood that I too could participate in the Twitter chat related to the conference just by including the designated hashtag (which, again, always starts with "#") anywhere in my 140-character or less message.

Over the next two days at the conference, I shared my own thoughts and reflections about the sessions I attended and deeper connections I was making. That was great, but what was really exciting, for me, was how the Twitter feed allowed me to read the fleeting thoughts of those attending a session two doors down which I would, otherwise, be completely unable to access. There was actually more than one time when I chose to leave one session and join another because I could tell, from the Tweets, that it was more relevant to my own needs. I also found it rather interesting (and still do) when I find myself sitting in a room reading the Tweets of other people in the room with me. I find myself peering around trying to find out who is saying what—often because I think their ideas are intriguing and I want to hear more!

Since my entry into the Twitterverse, I've also had many opportunities to engage in conference backchannels that I couldn't attend in person. As I sit at home in my office, I can read the Tweets of those I follow who are at a conference on the other side of the country. This is always fun and offers an opportunity to glean resources and engage in some dialogue with educators who are physically present at the event. Walls are no longer barriers in a participatory society. In fact, now when I jump into a conference backchannel and recognize a user's name, I almost always respond with, "Are you here?" Attending face-to-face conferences has become an exciting opportunity for me to meet the individuals who I follow on Twitter and who regularly contribute to my lifelong learning.

TIP

Get Connected With Twitter Hashtags

Getting familiar with commonly used Twitter hashtags is a helpful way for you to find information relevant to your interests. Enter any hashtag into the "search" box on Twitter.com and you'll retrieve a feed of all the most recent Tweets sent with that hashtag.

If you'd like to designate a hashtag for your own class, college campus, or department all you have to do is determine the precise group of characters you'd like to use. It's a good idea to plug it into the Twitter search box to be sure it's not a popular one already—that is, unless contributions from the Twitter community might improve your dialogue. Also keep in mind, hashtags are not like URLs. You cannot "own" one. There's always a chance another group may begin to use it, so shoot for something unique if exclusivity is important to you.

If you're building your Twitter network and looking to engage in some education-related chat, here are a few popular hashtags you may want to try out. These are not higher ed specific.

- **#onlinelearning**—chat about online learning
- **#edtech**—Tweets related to technology in education
- **#engchat**—English
- **#highered**—news and events related to college and universities
- **#mathchat**—math
- **#historyteacher**—history
- **#flipclass**—resources related to the flipped classroom model (see Introduction)
- **#iPadChat**—use of iPads (not specific to education)
- **#assistivetech**—news about assistive technologies
- **#elearning**—web-enhanced or online learning
- **#followfriday**—a fun way to recognize Twitter users, known as "tweeps" in the Twitterverse, who have inspired you (use only on Fridays)
- **#mlearning** and **#mobilelearning**—messages about mobile learning

TIP

Use Existing Public Lists to Jumpstart the Development of Your Personal Learning Network

As noted above, you won't experience the most beneficial aspects of using Twitter for lifelong learning until you have established a community of users you want to follow. You'll know you're on the right track when you start getting excited about the terrific resources you receive each time you peek at your Twitter feed.

In addition to searching for individual users with Twitter's "who to follow" tool (http://twitter.com/who_to_follow), you can also lean on the Twitter community for some help getting started. As noted earlier, Twitter gives you the option to organize your "tweeps"

Figure 5.1 Twitter screenshot. Used with permission from Catherine Hillman in accordance with Twitter's guidelines.

(Twitter lingo for users in your network) into "lists" which are, essentially, like groups. When a user creates a list, s/he may mark it as public or private. Public lists are viewable on a user's Twitter profile and any user can follow a public list with the click of a button.

So, as you start following people, take note of who provides you with great ideas (these may include comments, quotes or links to articles, tools, and/or blog posts). Click on a user's name to go to the user's homepage and then click "View full profile." You will see a feed of their most recent Tweets in the right column and in the left column, you'll see a menu of content options you may choose from. Click on "Lists" to view the lists this user has subscribed to. In the right column, you will see the names of the lists. You may click on each one to view the users who make up the list and, if it is a public list, you may "subscribe" to it yourself or follow any of the individual users.

Listorious.com is also a useful tool for locating pre-curated Twitter lists, as well as individual Twitter users who share your interests. If you're still leery about Twitter, do a couple of searches on Listorious using keywords to describe your teaching discipline. You may discover a goldmine!

SHOWCASE

Catherine Hillman, who teaches Social Media for Marketing at Cuesta College, gives her students an activity that requires them to use Twitter to locate and follow 50 experts in a topic related to their interests. The activity engages students with Twitter as a learning resource and facilitates a meaningful relationship with social media that extends well beyond the superficial application social media tools typically play in the lives of students. Through the activity, students learn how to mine Twitter for relevant content and evaluate the Tweets in their feed using a process that Hillman refers to as "Signal-to-Noise" ratio: determine whose posts provide relevant information for your interests ("Signal") and eliminate those whose posts are not relevant to you ("Noise"). To view the lesson plan for Hillman's "Follow Fifty" activity (shared with a Creative Commons license) refer to the Chapter 5 online resources at: http://www.teachingwithemergingtech.com.

The Backchannel: Teaching in a Participatory Classroom

Trying to get more students to participate is a common struggle for college professors. "No matter what I do, it's always the same students who raise their hands." Sound familiar? Well, be careful what you wish for! Social media is making some sweeping changes in how, when, and where people participate.

With a cell phone connected to Twitter, learning from and with people anywhere in the world is literally just a few clicks away. According to Twitter, in September

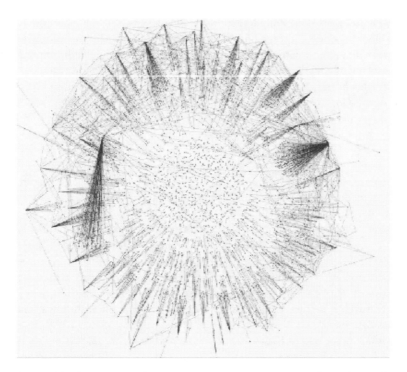

Figure 5.2 Twitter visualization. Printed with permission from André Panisson with credit to the Computer Science Department of the University of Turin and the ISI Foundation in Turin.

2011, the company had more than 100 million active users and half of these people log in every day. How many Tweets does that equate to? About a billion each week. About 40% of Twitter users log in just to listen to what the users in their feed are tweeting about and about 55% of users chime in from a mobile device. Additionally, 99% of the top 200 non-profits are active on Twitter.[1]

In 2011, the world witnessed an empowering effect of social media as Egyptians shared their experiences with the world via Twitter from the street corners of Cairo. Mobile technology and social media assisted Egyptian revolutionaries with organizing and sharing their experiences, reactions, and dreams about the future with the world in real-time with text, pictures, and video.

The impact that Mubarak's resignation announcement on February 11, 2011 had on the Twitterverse was captured by André Panisson with a cutting edge visualization technology as part of an international research study. The video (which can be viewed on YouTube at: http://youtu.be/2guKJfvq4uI) translates each Tweet sent with the hashtag #Jan25, which became synonymous with messages referencing events of the revolution, into a tiny node and as each Tweet is "retweeted" (forwarded by a user on to his/her own network), the node blossoms into a burst of more nodes. The video is fascinating to watch, as it illustrates the speed at which information can travel around the world with a mobile, social media tool like Twitter but it also offers each of us an opportunity to see a visual representation of what participatory learning looks like.

In 2011, Twitter also contributed to the demise of New York Congressman Anthony Weiner's political career after he mistakenly shared an inappropriate photograph with his public Twitter feed. Twitter flattens the playing field, distributing power to all and giving members of the community the opportunity to hold each user accountable for his or her actions. Introducing Twitter into the classroom rocks the foundations of "the lecture," as a "presentation" is no longer linear and the flow of questions and comments are no longer controllable by a single, authoritative figure. Again, this is why we began with a focus on "community" and "community ground-rules" in Chapter 1.

The phone in a person's hand is a symbol of our new participatory society. Multimedia content creation and global engagement are now in our pockets. Feature phones—a term that simply refers to a mobile phone without an internet connection—and smartphones both have the capability to send and receive Tweets (which may be written messages, snapshots, or, in more and more instances, videos). Feature phones can be easily connected to a user's Twitter account using SMS text messaging. What this means to you is that your students' fleeting ideas and questions that used to be silent and unobtrusive now bubble to the surface when phones are used as learning tools in a classroom. The result is a "backchannel." And, as many people are discovering at conferences as well as in the classroom, that backchannel can occur with or without your acknowledgment.

Cliff Atkinson, author of *The Backchannel: How Audiences are Using Twitter and Social Media and Changing Presentations Forever*, defines a backchannel as "a line of communication created by people in an audience to connect with others inside or outside the room, with or without the knowledge of the speaker at the front of the room. Usually facilitated by Internet technologies, it is spontaneous, self-directed, and limited in time to the duration of a live event."[2] Backchannels are not specific to Twitter-usage but they are a phenomenon that has been influenced through the popularization of social media and the use of mobile devices. While the idea of a backchannel may make you uncomfortable and even offer one more reason to ban cell phones from your classroom, some professors think they hold opportunities for improving classroom learning.

For many years, Clicker Response Systems (commonly referred to as "clickers") have been used in college classrooms to increase student engagement and assess student learning at various points during a lecture—and they're still around and still being used. Clickers require students to have access to a particular device that grants them the ability to contribute a response to a question or questions that their instructor created before class with the necessary software. These systems are often proprietary and require equipment to be purchased or leased, by the institution or by students, and the software must be licensed. Clickers give professors more control over the contributions made by students by granting them the power to create questions to which students respond, often in multiple-choice format. A "backchannel," on the other hand, captures all the fleeting ideas from the group of students in a classroom.

For this reason, professors often write the backchannel concept off as a learning distraction, based on the idea that students can't be paying attention if they're typing a message on a cell phone. This makes me scratch my head, as professors stress the importance of notetaking during lectures. How are these two activities cognitively different? Concerns about students mocking a professor also contribute to the controversies around the backchannel.

Derek Bruff, a senior lecturer and director of the Center for Teaching at Vanderbilt University and author of *Teaching With Classroom Response System: Creating Active Learning Environments*, theorizes that backchannel tools offer opportunities to enhance the type of student engagement clickers initiate. He considers participating in a backchannel as a form of "active listening." Drawing from his own experiences, Bruff reflects, "When I attend a keynote talk at a conference, I'll often Tweet about the most interesting points made by the speaker, and I'll sometimes respond to comments made about the talk by others on the backchannel. That's not some form of distraction or even multitasking—it's active listening. I think it's great that teachers are encouraging students to listen actively in similar ways in the classroom."[3]

Some professors, like Bruff, are stepping out to test the waters of backchannels and explore how this new social terrain can be used to support, rather than derail, learning. From my experiences, what these professors have in common is an interest in increasing student participation in a class (physical or online) and a sensitivity to the fact that while many students feel completely comfortable asking questions in a lecture setting, others (most) will never speak up—out of fear of sounding stupid, or feeling inadequate (maybe the student feels badly about her accent or was responded to in a poor manner by a professor in another class), or due to a cognitive learning disorder that simply makes him learn at a different pace. These are the students who are more likely to tune out and be challenged in a traditional lecture environment. Backchannel tools can provide more options for students to participate, as opposed to acting as a replacement for the verbal dialogue in a class.

SHOWCASE

The Twitter Experiment

Dr. Monica Rankin, professor of history at UT Dallas, was an early adopter of Twitter in the classroom for a backchannel tool. Her work is showcased in a brief and informative video on YouTube titled "The Twitter Experiment" (http://youtu.be/6WPVWDkF7U8) that was produced by Kim Smith, a grad student in Emerging Media and Communications at UT Dallas. With help from her TA, Megan Malone, Rankin established a Twitter hashtag and encouraged her students to use their laptop or cell phone to send Tweets. Rankin's 90-student class met three times each week: twice for a lecture and once, on Fridays, for a quiz and discussion. The use of Twitter was encouraged after the quiz each Friday.

Rankin notes that she had many students who didn't know what Twitter was and had to set up accounts. Despite being encouraged to do so before class, most waited until class time to take care of this step. The first two weeks of Twitter activity was mostly "start up" content ("test, test"; "How does this work?"; etc.) with a few meaningful Tweets. This is an important point, as there is always a "start up" period with using new technologies in a class and I think instructors who understand this will plan for it, rather than view it as a nuisance, and will be more successful with their instructional goals.

Rankin acknowledges that her experiment required her to reassess things week-by-week and try new things. She found that the Tweets became more insightful and the in-class discussions became more dynamic when students were placed into small groups of 3–5 and given a topic to discuss (verbally). The groups were instructed to identify the "best" ideas and Tweet them for the rest of the class to engage their contributions.

Throughout the discussions, the Twitter stream with the students' contributions (with use of a Twitter "search widget") was projected on a large screen in front of the class and students with internet access could open it and view it on their own laptop or smartphone. Rankin also observed that, like most small group activities, the quality increased the more she and her TA circulated around the classroom and checked in with groups to facilitate their ideas.

Malone, Rankin's TA, noted that the experiment was exciting because typically in a discussion there are only 3–4 students who willingly participate and with Twitter this number increased tenfold. Additionally, having the Tweets available online enabled her to go back and follow up with the students' Tweets over the weekend with the option to send them a "direct message" (or DM) which is a private exchange on Twitter. Bobby Sibert, a student featured in Rankin's video, points out that the Tweets shared by his classmates became a valuable study resource after class, as well.

There were challenges, of course, including the 140-word limitation imposed on each Tweet. But Rankin realizes that Twitter isn't the best tool for discussion of complex ideas; rather, it should be theorized as a tool that students can use *when* they have an idea or question appropriate for a Tweet, as opposed to when it's appropriate to engage in a verbal conversation with their class peers. Moreover, she observes that requiring students to limit their ideas to 140 characters forces the students to filter their ideas and think about what they want to say and how to best say it in a succinct way. Twitter forcing students to focus? Hmmm. That's an interesting twist.

Rankin also accommodated students who didn't have a cell phone or laptop by allowing them to hand write their comments and give them to the TA who would post them to the feed after class was over. Additionally, in one instance, she engaged the Twitter stream of student comments while she was out of state traveling at a conference. As her TA conducted the discussion in person, Rankin chimed in on the feed, "Your instructor is present," and participated virtually in the exchanges. Again, walls are no longer barriers to participation!

Tools for Participatory Learning Environments

Participatory learning is the form of learning that occurs through interactions with social media, like Twitter, Facebook, and YouTube. As the popularity and daily use of social media continues to increase, participatory learning is reshaping the way we learn. Learning is participatory when the outcome is a product that has been constructed through contributions made by members of a group or community.

In *The Future of Thinking*, Cathy Davidson and David Theo Goldberg use participatory learning synonymously with "digital learning" and examine how it challenges many hallmarks of academia. "With digital learning, the play between technology, composer, and audience is no longer passive . . . In conventional learning institutions, the lines of authorship and authority are clearly delineated, and the place of teacher, student, and technology are well known. With digital learning, these conventional models of authority break down."[4]

Transitioning into a participatory learning environment can be nerve racking for a professor, as I reflected in the introduction where I share my "flipped classroom" experiment. When you've been positioned as the one with the answers whose responsibility it is to pass information on to students and ensure they *know* it, facilitating a participatory learning environment may make you feel as if the stable ground beneath you is crumbling away. My advice is to remember that your role is still *essential*. It's not any less important, just different.

To understand how I integrate participatory learning in my own classes, visualize a spectrum with "accessing content" at one end and "contributing content" at the other. If each of my students' learning experiences could be tracked visually on this continuum, the node representing their actions would continually shift from left to right: from accessing to contributing, back to accessing, then again to contributing. In my learning units, students begin by accessing information in a multitude of formats (videos, articles, chapters, images, audio, either created by me, provided as part of the course materials, created by the students in a previous unit, or a combination of all three) and then apply what they've learned in participatory learning activities (creating and commenting on blog posts, commenting in and adding slides to a VoiceThread, collaboratively producing Google presentations, etc.).

Each student understands that his/her goal is to master the learning objectives for that particular unit. After a student has accessed the assigned content and made the required contributions, they "access" the contributions made by their peers—looping back to the opposite end of the spectrum—and then leave comments and feedback-looping back again. As students regularly contribute their own content (in response to the activities I have designed) and interact with the student-generated content to deconstruct, discuss, apply, analyze it, the more *participatory* the learning environment is.

The following pages offer a selection of tools that offer potential for participatory learning and several practical examples of how professors are using them to innovate their teaching approaches.

TIP

A Simple Analogy for Understanding Microblogging

Microblogging takes its name from the idea that it is a miniaturized version of a blog. A blog is like an online journal and a great tool for sharing reflective, critical, or creative writing with peers. A microblog is like a sticky note; providing a method for sharing brief ideas, reflections, questions, or links to online resources (blog posts, articles, videos, images, etc.). Twitter, discussed above in the context of backchannels, is a microblogging tool, as are HootCourse and Wiggio (discussed below).

PollEverywhere

   http://www.polleverywhere.com

Feature Overview

- Free and premium accounts.
- Special pricing available for higher ed accounts.
- Create polls that students can respond to with text messaging, a smartphone, web browser, or Twitter. Display results in live time, projected from a website.
- Download poll results in .CSV format.
- Project polls from the web or insert them into a Powerpoint or Keynote presentation.
- Free accounts limit each poll to 40 responses.
- Premium account provides the option to restrict responses only to invited members of a group.
- With a premium account, you can organize students into groups for competitive quizzes.

Sandra C. Haynes, an art history professor at Pasadena City College, uses PollEverywhere in her large lecture classes. With her free account, she can easily create simple, single-question polls with a multiple-choice or open-ended response and build them into her lecture presentations. When it's time for a poll, her students know the drill—they whip out a cell phone or use a laptop or smartphone to respond to the poll. After a 30-second pause for responses to be collected, the responses are tallied and presented in a visual format on the screen for both Haynes and her students to see.

PollEverywhere is an updated version of a classroom response system (aka "clickers") but this solution doesn't require students or the instructor to purchase (or lease) clickers or remember to bring them to class. Rather, students are empowered to use their existing mobile devices as learning tools. PollEverywhere is an attractive tool, "because it does not require students to have a smartphone or a laptop, which many community college students do not own," says Haynes. And while the 40-person limit for a free poll sounded like a challenge to me, Haynes responded quite differently, explaining that her students are aware that not every vote will be recorded so the response limitation actually creates a kind of lively competition within the classroom. Aside from having the opportunity to engage her students and check in on their learning throughout a lecture, Haynes says she also loves using the tool because it's a great feeling to see students get so excited about being encouraged to use their cell phones in class!

HootCourse

 http://www.hootcourse.com

Feature Overview

- Free, secure microblogging tool.
- Create your own "course" area for private interactions.
- Invite students to your course with a simple invitation link.
- Access granted with an existing Facebook or Twitter account.
- Messages up to 140 characters in length may be sent from an internet equipped device (laptop or smartphone browser).
- Users have the option to share a post privately or also have it be viewable publicly on their Twitter or Facebook page.

HootCourse is a microblogging tool which is similar to Twitter in that it provides an easy method for sending messages (from an internet equipped device) up to 140 characters in length.

But it differs from Twitter in a few important ways—HootCourse is a microblogging tool that adds a layer of privacy to classroom interactions and streamlines the account creation process. To get started with using HootCourse, a professor simply creates a new course and is quickly provided with an invitation link to share with students. That link can then be shared with students in a course management system or via email and once a student clicks on the link, she is automatically taken to a page and asked to sign into HootCourse using either her Facebook or Twitter credentials. This streamlines the account creation process a bit, as nearly all college students have a Twitter *or* Facebook account and using HootCourse eliminates the need to create *another* account.

Only members of a course (or, in other words, a person who has clicked on the invite link) will have access to an individual course in HootCourse and if a user is a member of multiple courses then HootCourse creates a dashboard for you to select the course in which you wish to interact.

SHOWCASE

PollEverywhere + HootCourse = Increased Engagement and Accountability

Corbette Doyle, a lecturer in Leadership, Policy, and Organizations at Vanderbilt University, requires her students to use HootCourse to submit a question prior to coming to class. The question is based on a course-related topic she has shared in their course management system. She positions this activity as the students' "entrance ticket" to each class. Doyle had previously required students to respond to questions using clickers but wanted to refresh this approach to foster more critical thinking and student engagement.

Steph Milnes, Doyle's TA, was tasked with triaging the messages and identifying six Tweets that would be considered for class discussion topics. While only six Tweets are selected from each batch, all of them are graded with a simple rubric: 0 for missing, plagiarized, or unfamiliar with the material to 2.5 for excellent or above and beyond. Doyle then listed the six questions and had students vote on their favorite.

The voting process posed a little glitch in the flow of the activity, as HootCourse does not include the option to "favorite" Tweets (like Twitter does). If it had, students could easily vote that way. To remedy this, Doyle turned to PollEverywhere (see above). Doyle agrees that PollEverywhere is more effective than traditional clicker tools because there are always students who forget to bring their clickers to class but it's rare to find a student who forgets his phone!

Figure 5.3
HootCourse
screenshot. Printed
with permission from
HootCourse and
Corbette Doyle.

All in all, Doyle has been impressed with the quality of questions her students contribute. And, according to Milnes, the use of a Twitter-like tool makes assignments more appealing to students. She reflects:

> Reading the syllabus and seeing that you have to post a question on the readings before *every* class may initially seem daunting to students. Tweeting the questions though, certainly makes this task more appealing and accessible to students . . . I have heard from multiple students that they think its "cool" that they not only get to use their cell phones in class, but they get to use social media . . . for educational purposes. The perception is that Professor Doyle "gets them."[5]

But there's one more element of Doyle's innovative teaching practice that I find compelling. She reflects on how the flat, non-hierarchic feed within HootCourse results in students having greater accountability for their work when compared to the nested organization of a threaded-discussion. As she explains, "Public accountability is limited [in a discussion forum] by the fact that students must click on their peers' post to read it—the content is not readily available." Sometimes there are unexpected benefits to trying new tools!

Wiggio

 http://www.wiggio.com

Feature Overview:

- Free, secure microblogging tool.
- Create private groups for communications.
- Invite students with an invitation link or email addresses.
- Each group includes three interaction areas:
    — Feed: start a new conversation or reply to an existing one, add a file or link, schedule an event, start a live chat, initiate a virtual meeting with a whiteboard, and more!
    — Folder: a shared repository for online documents. Add existing files and links or create online documents and spreadsheets.
    — Calendar: a collaborative calendar on which group members may add important dates and events.
- Mobile app available.
- At the time of writing, Wiggio is free. The site notes that there are plans to offer a premium version. There is no clarity about which features will or may become premium features.

Many professors I've worked with really like the interactivity of Twitter but feel restricted by its public nature. If you find yourself in that category, check out Wiggio.

Wiggio (the "Wig" stands for "Work In Groups") blends the ease of a Twitter-like microblogging platform with a private group space and a grand infusion of collaboration. Inviting students to join your Wiggio group is as simple as sharing a link within your course management system or website and the features you'll find within your group are impressive.

Beyond the basics of microblogging, group members can also send voice and video memos to each other and opt to send text messages to group members who have connected a mobile phone to their account. Group members also have access to a virtual meeting tool that supports up to ten people and includes screensharing, a valuable resource for students who are working on group projects or study groups, as well as professors who are facilitating online tutor sessions. Additional features include polls and surveys, chat rooms, document hosting, and to-do-lists to assist with group management tasks.

VoiceThread

 http://www.voicethread.com

Feature Overview (Also Included in Chapter 4)

- Free and premium accounts with many options specific to higher ed, including site-wide licenses.
- Create asynchronous, online conversations around media (presentations, images, videos, and more).
- Students may leave comments in voice (with a microphone or phone), video (with a webcam), or text.
- Share with a link or embed on a website/course management system.
- Privacy settings include secure, semi-private, and public.
- While commenting, users use their mouse (or finger, on the mobile app) to annotate on the media shared in the center of a slide and when that comment is played back by another user, the annotation plays in sync with the user's voice.
- Free mobile app available.

VoiceThread is a tool that I have used in my classes since 2007. It has become integral to my online teaching and has also played a big role in changing the way I have taught my face-to-face classes too (see the Introduction for a reflection of my "flipped classroom" experiment featuring VoiceThread). In Chapter 4, we explored how VoiceThread can be used to foster personalized communications with your students and share content with them, but that's just the tip of the iceberg. VoiceThread also holds great potential for fostering participatory learning in an online, web-enhanced, or hybrid class.

VoiceThread is asynchronous or "time shifted" yet accommodates voice and video comments which are more commonly found in synchronous or "live" web conferencing applications (like Blackboard Collaborate, Adobe Connect, and others). When I create a VoiceThread, I view it as a learning activity—I include a title slide, a

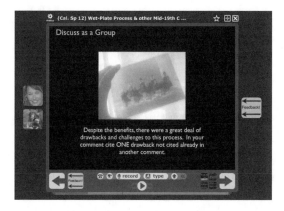

Figure 5.4 Screenshot of a slide from one of my VoiceThread learning activities. Used with permission from VoiceThread, Kim Plowright, author of the glass plate negative photograph, and Kellye Mills.

"Tips for VoiceThread" slide, a slide about grading criteria, and "Instruction" slides that explain precisely what students are expected to do in the VoiceThread. Sometimes I follow these introductory slides with a screencast video I've created (like a mini-lecture) and then I upload slides following the video that contain text-based prompts and images tied back to their reading and the instructional video in the VoiceThread. The students are expected to leave their comments on the "prompt" slides. The prompts may ask them to summarize a historical photographic process, identify drawbacks or advantages one process had over another, compare and contrast images, analyze historical problems, interpret photographs, or collaboratively summarize contributions made by particular photographers covered in the unit.

I leave it to the students to choose which slides to comment on and I purposely include more slides than necessary, building in options for students and eliminating redundancy in the contributions. After leaving a comment, the student's profile image appears along the side of the media. Any user can click on the image to play the comment or click the "play" icon at the bottom and sit back as the slide plays like a movie. Listen, read, and watch the comments play—filled with the warmth of your students' presence! As the facilitator, I can easily leave "feedback" comments, which I do using a unique avatar or "identity" within my VoiceThread account. Each VoiceThread account can accommodate many "identities," allowing you to clearly call out your presence on a slide. I also have identity labeled "Sample Comment" that I use in complex activities so students know exactly what I expect of them.

The "Doodle" tool in VoiceThread is also especially appealing, as it turns each slide into a collaborative whiteboard. For example, in an online art appreciation class, students may be required to view a work of art and, while commenting, use the Doodle tool (activated by using a mouse with the web app or a finger/stylus with the mobile app) to circle an example of an implied line. Simultaneously, in a voice comment, they explain how the implied line they've circled contributes to guiding the viewer's eye through the image (follow this link to see a video demonstrating this activity: http://youtu.be/yC1NiyOB10A). Essentially, with the Doodle tool, any slide in a VoiceThread becomes a canvas on which you *and* your students can demonstrate mastery of skills.

What's also important to understand is that these learning activities in VoiceThread are peer-to-peer so the students are doing more than submitting an assignment, they are working together to create content from which the group learns.

VoiceThread has also been an exceptional tool for creating a sense of community in an online class. In 2008 I surveyed 101 of my online students (and received an 88% response rate). Eighty-two percent of the students strongly agreed or agreed that they are more motivated to succeed when they feel like they are part of a community in an online class. Eighty percent of students strongly agreed or agreed that VoiceThread contributed to establishing a sense of community in the class.[6]

Moreover, by using VoiceThread's group feature I have also granted my students "edit" access to a VoiceThread in an effort to allow them to add their own slides with their own media. I call the activity "Visual Thinking" and it is designed to be a student-generated presentation about mid-20th-century photographers but after the presentation is done, the student re-engage with it and learn from each others' contribution. The mid-20th century is a period that includes a vast array of photographers and in a traditional teaching environment, I am left to choose which photographers the students will learn about. In an effort to make the instruction more student-centered, I make a list of photographers and shared them on a Google Doc (see below for more info). The students access the editable document and sign up for the photographer they wanted to learn more about. Then they proceed to do research about the photographer using Google Books (http://books.google.com/) and locate two online images by the photographer using Google Image Search (http://www.google.com/imghp). After completing the research, their task is to "edit" the VoiceThread and add two slides pertaining to the photographer they chose, each slide displaying one photograph. The first slide is required to include a 400–500 word comment (I require voice or video comments in this activity) that answers the question, "Why is this photographer's work remembered today?" The first slide also has to include a text comment with the citation for the Google Book used in the research. The second slide (containing the second photograph) is designed to be a discussion prompt, written by the student.

After the first week of "Visual Thinking", the VoiceThread transforms from a presentation comprised of my introductory and "sample" slides (provided to model my expectations to my students) to a robust presentation of the work of 25 mid-20th century photographers. The second week of the activity requires the students to revisit the VoiceThread, learn about two other photographers, and respond, in voice, to the related discussion prompts. Then the students circle over to their blog (in Ning, see later in this chapter for more information) and write a post reflecting on what they learned about the photographers they selected in week two and how the design of the activity allowed them to take control of their learning. It is common for students to note an appreciation for being able to select the photographers who are important to them. Students also expressed that they learned from the challenges they encountered and the need to work through their problems. Some students even noted that they had a newfound appreciation for the amount of work their professors go through to develop their lecture content!

TIP

Locate existing videos for your VoiceThreads

A single VoiceThread can hold a variety of media filetypes (images, videos, PDFs, and more). To use a video in your VoiceThread, it is best to have the file saved to your computer. But understanding how to locate existing videos that have been shared with permission for users to download and re-use them and that are formatted perfectly for use in a VoiceThread is no simple feat. I recommend Vimeo.com.

To find a video, go to vimeo.com and enter your search terms in the search box at the top and click the search icon. When the results return, click on "Show Advanced Filters." In the "Filters" box, select "is downloadable" and your results will be filtered to only show videos that you have access to download. Click on a video and then click on the "Download" button. Click on the icon for the preferred video size for your project (free VoiceThread accounts permit file uploads up to 25MB and PRO accounts increase this to 100MB) and it will download to your computer.

Visit the Chapter 5 area of the Online Resources site at www.teachingwithemergingtech. com to view a video demonstrating this search process.

SHOWCASE

Penn State Takes VoiceThread Campus-Wide!

Site licenses for web-based, emerging technologies are not quite mainstream yet but in 2010 Penn State University adopted VoiceThread for use by more than 94,000 faculty and students. By integrating VoiceThread with their single-sign-on authentication system, faculty and students are automatically provided with a VoiceThread account (eliminating the need to require students to set up their own account at the start of a class). Students receive an upgraded Basic account which allows them to create up to 50 VoiceThreads (a free account is limited to just three). This opens many exciting possibilities for using VoiceThread for student-generated projects in support of course and program outcomes like ePortfolios, interviews with subject-matter experts, online presentations, debates with peers, and it expands the options for assessing language skills online. View Penn State's VoiceThread support site at: http://voicethread.psu.edu.

Facebook

 http://www.facebook.com

Feature Overview

- A free social network.
- Share status updates, images, videos, and links with your Friends or within a Group (with a range of privacy settings).
- Create a Page to promote a business, institution, cause, product, organization or for your own class.
- Free mobile app.

Teaching with Facebook is a most interesting topic to write about because it is the tool that is used most by both students and professors. For that reason, it's a natural choice as there's no need to spend much time explaining how to use it. However, integrating Facebook into your teaching can also be a treacherous endeavor. If you are a college professor and use Facebook for your personal life, you probably have some type of personal policy about how to respond to Friend requests from students. I, for example, do not accept friend requests from my current students. I have accepted Friend requests from prior students if they were students with whom I had an interest in staying in touch. I use a lot of personal discretion in this area. These decisions are important because anyone in your "Friends" network usually has access to the content you share on Facebook (although there are options for filtering this content). You need to think about the repercussions: Is it a good idea for your students to read your posts about your teaching frustrations or see images from your summer trip to Fiji? Facebook does provide the option to filter who can see each status update you make, including selecting from custom lists you have arranged but this gets cumbersome and it's easy to forget to make this selection before sharing an update.

So, then, why is Facebook worth considering as a teaching tool? For one, the Groups feature is an attractive option for creating a space for your students to connect—or simply encourage your students to create *their own* Facebook group for the class (or part of the class). Chances are, you'll find a student who is excited and motivated about taking on that task. Creating a group is free and provides the creator with three privacy settings: Secret (only members can see the group and its content), Closed (anyone can see the group in a search within Facebook but only members can see posts made inside it), and Open (anyone can see the group, as well as the posts within it).

Members of a group can post brief updates (like in Twitter or Wiggio), ask questions, share photos and links to web resources. At any time, group members who are online can engage in chat and there are options for sharing documents and scheduling group events too.

There are many other strategies for using Facebook to support your students' teaching too. For example:

- Give your students a topic and ask them to poll their Facebook network for answers and then use the results to stimulate a discussion.
- Have your students "like" a Page dedicated to a public figure, organization, or product and analyze the content that is shared and the comments made by the other followers.
- Encourage your students to analyze what their Friends are saying about a current news story and discuss these perceptions with the class or write a blog post reflecting on them.
- Have students "like" a politician's Facebook page and analyze the content that gets shared there. Discuss with your students what can be learned about the politician's viewpoints and positions from the information shared and the users who support him/her.

Ning

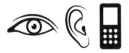   http://www.ning.com

Feature Overview

- Premium-only service.
- Create your own private or public social network.
- A Ning Mini, the least expensive account, costs less than $5 per month and offers a fully private social network that you customize with your own title and theme.
- Invite students to join your private network with a simple invitation link.
- Customizable profile questions include private questions which can be used to increase your one-on-one communication with students at the start of a term.
- All members are provided with their own wall that includes an array of features (which you can enable or disable) including a personalized profile image, a blog, a box for adding a status update, a block for uploading images and videos (which supports the embedding of YouTube videos by pasting a link into a box), and a list of recent activity.
- Mobile app available for iPhone.

Ning provides an opportunity for anyone to create a social network about anything! For educators, this translates to an easy way to create an engaging, peer-to-peer learning environment that can be customized with a dazzling array of options. Once a member of a Ning network, a user can post micro-blog updates (similar to those shared in Twitter, HootCourse, and Wiggio), add images, share videos from YouTube, and add posts to a blog that is built-in to your very own homepage in Ning.

The blog feature makes Ning attractive to many professors, as it's easy to use and supports multimedia in addition to text, which can make writing more engaging for students. Students can easily interact with each other by clicking on the Blogs tab at the top and viewing recent posts made by their peers and leaving comments for each other.

Figure 5.5 Ning screenshot. Used with permission from Ning

Moreover, it's very feasible to blend Ning into a course that is taught primarily with a course management system. For example, I teach a class in Blackboard and students enter the course every week, click on a button titled Learning Units, access the new unit, and review their assignments. Within the unit's folder, they will find an announcement from me (in video and text), the unit's learning objectives, reading assignments and sometimes videos to watch. Then they have one or two activities in which to participate. One of these activities is usually a blog post in our Ning network (which is a secure network to which only students have access).

The students receive the prompt, which usually has a 500-word minimum, for the post in Blackboard and they are encouraged to write the post in a word processing app (to take advantage of spell check and the word count tool). The blog posts are often written about particular images, as I teach art history, and the students are also instructed to embed the image within the post in Ning, to ensure their ideas are illustrated (see later in this chapter to learn how I use Pinterest to point students to suggested images). After the post is written, the students simply click on the "Ning" button in our Blackboard course menu (which is set up as an external link). A new window opens with a log-in screen for Ning. They log in, click on the "My Page" tab to be taken to their individual blog, create a new blog post, paste the essay into the text box, add the image, and publish the post.

Students can easily review the blog posts their peers have written and leave comments too by clicking on the "Blogs" tab at the top of any page in Ning. An effective way to make commenting part of the learning is to include criteria in the post for students to reflect on questions they still have about the topic they're writing about. Then at the start of the next unit, include an assignment for students to log into Ning and leave a comment on one other blog post (preferably one that does not yet have a comment) responding to at least one question in the post. I see a lot of energy and self-motivation in students when they're prompted to help each other solve questions. Usually, the problem solving ends up being more of a back and forth discussion, "Here's what I think. What do you think?"

The higher end Ning account options include more features that are highly desirable in a class setting, including groups which provide partitioned areas for students to organize and collaborate about a topic or project and customizable pages within the network which allow you to, essentially, build out your network into a robust website.

Ning is also a terrific enhancement to a course management system because it provides an environment that supports the embedding of widgets that can be difficult to integrate into some course management systems. For example, the homepage of your Ning network could include a Twitter search widget displaying recent Tweets including your course's hashtag, a Skype button communicating your status, and/or an EyeJot widget for students to send you an asynchronous video message.

I've found that the friendly environment of Ning seems to naturally encourage students to reach out and connect with each other, even add photographs of themselves, their friends, and family (although you should specify that this is not required so students who prefer not to share these items understand that's ok too)—right away it's clear to learners that Ning is a student-centered, rather than instructor-centered, learning environment. Ning extends students with the option to personalize their learning space, which, to me, seems like a natural thing to offer to learners who will be together in a class for up to 17 weeks! Could you imagine walking into a cubicle that you knew you'd be working in for an extended period of time and not being able to personalize it with your favorite things? How would that affect your productivity? Ning increases a student's interest in coming back to the class environment too because things are always changing—just like Facebook or YouTube.

SHOWCASE

Writing to Learn . . . with Ning!

Two graduate assistants at University of Connecticut have used Ning as a supplemental writing environment for their face-to-face French Literature and Civilization in Translation classes. Nathalie Ettzevoglou and Jessica McBride employ the "writing to learn" approach in their classes, which emphasizes the use of writing to both examine what a student understands, as well as a tool to stimulate learning and thinking critically.[7] This is not a new pedagogical approach; in fact, it has been around for decades. But the two were curious to see what would happen if they infused an old idea with a new technology. They asked, "Before the predominance of computers, write-to-learn activities usually consisted of informal writing journals that may or may not be shared with other students. Why not combine the traditional elements of a write-to-learn activity with the exciting possibilities available through technology, such as the addition of images, video, and global interaction?"[8]

Ning provided an ideal platform. After joining the network their professors established, the students used their individual blogs inside of Ning between class sessions. Each blog was like a canvas on which students could write personal reflections about discussions from class and critique each other's ideas. Since all the student blogs are accessible through the Ning network, it is more streamlined than using an external blogging tool (like Blogger or WordPress). With Ning, there is no need for an instructor to collect dozens of links to student's blogs. Rather, there is a single link to the Ning network that provides access to all of the student blogs.

While many college professors find privacy is a priority when evaluating and selecting web-based tools for their students, Ettzevoglou and McBride purposely elected to keep their Ning network open to the public. This choice was made because they believed the public blogging experience, opposed to the discussion forums in a course management system, would increase a students' sense of ownership over and accountability for one's work. Not only were students informed that the world was watching but global viewership was tracked and illustrated through the dynamic Clustrmap (http://www.clustrmaps.com/) embedded on the network's homepage. The Clustrmap showed a world map with groups of tiny red dots, representing internet users who had visited the Ning network, and a number at the top communicating the total number of visitors to date.

Students responded favorably to the experiment, noting an appreciation for Ning's uniqueness, the opportunity to engage a global audience in their learning, and customize their environment. One student shared:

> I found Ning to be something very different than I have used before in a class. Here at UCONN, we have the discussion boards on HuskyCT, but with Ning we were able to add people from all over who shared an interest in French Literature. Also, we were able to decorate our personal pages with our specific interests. I would say seeing what other people wrote in their posts helped my writing. I could also see a different perspective on the topic which helped me by knowing what other writing styles students were using.[9]

Students who participated agreed that the top three benefits of using Ning were:

- [It] gave them the opportunity to hear other opinions on the material covered in class.
- It helped them prepare for class discussions.
- It sparked new ideas for paper topics.[10]

Ettzevoglou and McBride agree and see Ning not only as a tool for promoting learning through writing but also an opportunity to make real-world ties to the curriculum and foster deep learning. They reflect, "We believe that this tool has effectively helped our students see the benefits of writing to learn in a way that would not have been possible with traditional activities or other web-based tools. Ning provides an environment in which our students can learn how to express themselves in writing and how to share their thoughts with others from all over the world."[11]

Google+

   http://www.google.com/+

Feature Overview

- Free social network.
- Connect with users, add them to customizable Circles.
- Each time you share content, select which Circle(s) will have access to it.
- Hangouts offer live one-on-one or group video chat with add-ons including integration of Google Docs and screensharing.
- Free mobile app.

Unveiled in beta form in June 2011, Google+ is making some impressive waves in the social media space, offering easy-to-manage privacy options that make it more useful and easier to teach with than Facebook. At the time of writing, the educators I spoke with who use Google+ for professional and personal networking agree that it's not quite ready for student use yet, as it is still considered to be in beta stage, but there's a lot of potential for implementation very soon.

Google+ is a social network, like Facebook. It's built-in to a Google account so if you have a Gmail account, have created a Google Calendar, Doc, or site then you have access to Google+. Getting started just involves creating your profile and adding other users to your "Circles." Circles are a feature that set Google+ apart from Facebook, which is the most widely used social network. You can create one, ten, or fifty Circles-and they are organic, allowing you to customize them at any time. In fact, you could even create a Circle on the fly for a specific use, for example, a student group project, and then delete it. For example, you could have a collection of Circles titled "family," "co-workers," "football," "kids' school," "innovative educators," "art historians," "Photo 130," etc. A circle could have three users in it or it could have 200. And users can appear in multiple circles or be included in just one.

When you share content on Google+ (which may be a link to an online resource, a text status update, or a photo), you decide which Circle(s) to share it with. It's a quick, seamless process, unlike the one built into Facebook. It's true that you can manage who sees your content in Facebook but it's a clunkier process, requiring you to organize Friends into "Lists" and then select how you want to share the content: with the public, only yourself (an option I haven't figured out an application for yet!), or select the "custom" option which allows you to share it with a single friend or select from one of your "Lists." To me, this process doesn't feel as fluid and organic as Google+ and I think it's due to the fact that Facebook is trying to re-do a process and workflow that is already established, while Google+ has designed an experience around the curation of one's Circles.

Circles are also used to initiate a Hangout in Google+. A Hangout is a live, media-rich interaction space that provides you with the ability to have video or text-chat with any user who joins your Hangout. The beauty here is folding your Hangouts in with your Circles. For example, if I create a Hangout in Google+, I decide which circles to announce it to. If I select "Photo 130" then all the users I have added to that circle will automatically see an update from me in their live feed that says I am "Hanging Out." Clicking on that update will take the user straight into the Hangout and extend the option to chat with me.

At the time of writing, Hangouts may be used with a set of beta features by selecting to start a "Hangout with Extras." If you select this option, the extra goodies that are folded into your hangout include:

- Hangouts with custom names.
- Integration of Google Docs, Notes and sketchpad, which facilitates live group collaboration.
- Screensharing, which can be used to demonstrate a concept or explain a process with your students.

While I see lots of potential for Google+ in education, there are still a few kinks that need to be smoothed out before I'll integrate it into a class. I really like the idea of using Hangouts for office hours. Although they don't support more than 10 video users at one time, it's rare for me to ever have that many students attend an online office hour so I think it would work well. The Google Docs integration (part of Hangouts with Extras) also provides a method of sharing a doc synchronously in a Hangout, facilitating options for one-on-one tutoring sessions or group project reviews.

But the challenge with using Google+ for teaching is finding a simple way to collect students into a Circle. There is just no easy way to do it. You can easily send an invitation link for new users to join Google+ but what I'd like to see is a link to join a Circle I create in Google+ which would allow existing users to click and be added and new users to join and be added. For now, the mechanics of getting started are a mixed bag—but things are quickly changing.

Other Google Apps

Using these apps will add an array of collaborative, participatory tools to your teaching. Each app listed below is part of the Google Apps suite. To use them, you must have a free Google account. They enable you to create content that you can share with selected users, anyone who has access to the link, or share it publicly. You may also invite collaborators to edit the content.

Google Docs: http://docs.google.com

- When you create a Google Doc, you may select any of the following formats: Document (a simple page), Presentation (like an online Powerpoint), Spreadsheet, Form (similar to a survey), Drawing, or Table.
- Your Docs may be organized into Collections that you can share with other users.
- Docs may be self-created and shared like static websites or you may choose to grant users with editing privileges, creating a fully collaborative space.
- Each doc may be kept private, shared with a select group of users, shared with anyone who has access to the link, or be made fully public.

TIP

Use Google Docs for Easy Group Management

Many instructors, like myself, use Google Docs for group management tasks. For example, in my class, I create topics for students to choose from for particular assignments. By listing the topics in a Google Doc spreadsheet and making the page editable to anyone who has access to the link, I can easily include the link in my course shell and allow students to simply type their name next to the topic of their choice. This empowers them to take control of the project, ensures the list is current, and removes me from the process of updating and managing the progress.

SHOWCASE

Create an Online Ice Breaker With a Collaborative Presentation

I use a Google Doc presentation for an ice breaker in my online History of Photography class. The project is titled "My Favorite Photograph" and it invites each student to edit a slide that I have created for them. Upon entering, they read a few preliminary instruction slides explaining how the assignment works, including an opportunity to watch a how-to video that illustrates how to edit the presentation. Then they locate the slide I have inserted with their name on it, add their favorite photograph and add text explaining why they've selected it. Slowly, throughout the first week of class, the empty presentation slides transform into a beautiful, meaningful collection of images generated by members of the class. The following week, the students return to the presentation and view the completed product. In a blog post, they reflect on what they learned about photographic meaning from this activity. The project is a fun, easy way to engage students in a collaborative activity the first week of class and also engages them in a critical inquiry about the nature of photographic meaning by engaging them with the diverse array of images selected by their peers—which usually include anything from old family photographs, snapshots of children, loved ones away at war, nature landscapes, and works of art. It's a perfect introduction to the class wrapped in an ice breaker that helps students get to know each other. Visit the Chapter 5 Showcase online resources for a PDF guide to creating your own collaborative Google Dec presentation.

Finally, if you have a collaborative project in your class (or on campus) in which you are still using a single document that gets edited by multiple people—stop! The most ideal use for Google Docs is to upload an existing document (an MS Word or Excel spreadsheet, for example), adjust the share settings to your preferences, and edit it with your peers. The edits are all collected in a single location and you can engage in chat with others who are editing the file when you are. In a Google Doc document, use the Comment feature to leave sticky note comments that other users can reply to—and you can mark as "resolved" once the loose ends are tied up.

Google Sites: http://sites.google.com

- Create websites for free.
- Easily insert images, videos, and other media options (calendars, Twitter widgets, a feed of your recent blog posts, weather status updates, and more) using the Google Gadgets.
- Share with individuals, anyone who has the link, or make fully public.
- You may also make a Site editable by other users.

TIP

Save Time by Starting With a Template!

Get off to a quick start by using one of the Google Site templates available at: http://sites.google.com/site/sitetemplateinfo/home.

I like creating a Google Site as a resource for conference presentations. Participants appreciate the ability to quickly reference an array of examples and resources I have collected on the Google Site at their own convenience.

Google Moderator: http://www.google.com/moderator/

- Gather ideas, suggestions, or questions about a topic (referred to as a "Series").
- You may allow users to vote for each other's submissions, providing a simple method for assessing a group of users' preferences, opinions, or coming to a consensus about a decision.
- Each series is shared with a simple link and can be made public on the web or visible only to those with a link.

SHOWCASE

Workshop Facilitation With Google Moderator

Derek Bruff recommends Google Moderator for facilitating Q&A at the end of a seminar or workshop. He notes that it can be a great way to have audience members submit questions or ideas and vote on those that are most relevant to the group. This allows the session presenter to spend the limited Q&A time responding to the questions that are most relevant to the audience.

It can also be used to facilitate group activities in a workshop or class. For example, while facilitating a workshop about using emerging tools in college teaching and learning, Bruff and his co-presenters encouraged the audience to break into small groups, ensuring at least one group member had an internet equipped device (required to add an idea to a Google Moderator topic).[12] He then asked each group to identify "roadblocks, obstacles, and

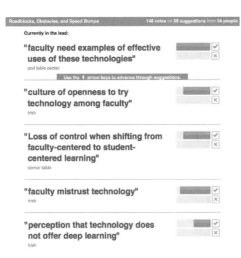

Figure 5.6 Google Moderator screenshot. Used with permission from Derek Bruff in accordance with Google's guidelines.

speedbumps" that are preventing change in education. Each group then entered their list of roadblocks into Google Moderator and when the breakout period had ended, Bruff encouraged the entire group to view the list online and vote for the roadblocks they felt their campus academic technology support group was best positioned to help them overcome. Standing in the front of the room, Bruff presented the results on the large screen for all to see. These results provided clear outcomes for the workshop and a great, effective wrap up to a group discussion!

Content Curation Tools

The tools shared below fall under the umbrella of content curation. A curator is a title granted to individuals employed in a museum whose responsibility it is to identify, select, and acquire objects for inclusion in exhibitions. Curation is a skill that requires an individual to be an expert on a particular topic to effectively assess and validate whether or not an object (or, in our case, an online resource) adds value to the overarching objectives of a collection. As our digital, mobile society continues to inspire and encourage users to create and share content, content curation continues to become an important 21st-century skill. The tools below can be used to require students to take on the role of a curator, which involves locating, assessing, validating resources relevant to a topic and sharing them in some creative ways. All in all, content curation is an area that is growing by leaps and bounds and many savvy web users are thinking about content curation as the next generation web search. That is, why enter a few search terms into a web search tool when you can search collections of resources hand selected by other users?

Delicious

 http://www.delicious.com

Feature Overview

- Free social bookmarking tool.
- Save websites online and organize them into groups with "tags."
- Choose to make each bookmark public or private.
- Public bookmarks can be retrieved from delicious.com by entering a tag into the search box.
- Easily share all your bookmarks or those tagged with one specific tag with a link.
- Curate a collection of bookmarks into a magazine-like arrangement called a Stack.
- Mobile bookmarklet is available (a bookmarklet is a link within your browser that you click on to add a site to your account).

If you've used the web, you're familiar with the value of using bookmarks to save, store, and organize web resources for later reference. Delicious makes bookmarking a social activity, allowing users to save bookmarks for later, make bookmarks accessible from any internet connected computer, organize their own bookmarks into categories using "tags," and opt to share them with others. Sharing your bookmarks online allows more users to peruse vetted websites about particular topics and also creates opportunities for students to work independently or together with a group to collaboratively curate a group of links around particular topics.

For example, I am a Delicious user and have tagged many web resources that relate to the various topics of this book. I've opted to share these resources publicly and you can access them in a variety of ways. For example, to view all the resources related to this book, you want to locate my delicious bookmarks that I've tagged with "bptet." To do so, just go to: http://www.delicious.com/brocansky/bptet. This URL simply points you to Delicious, my username, and the tag "bptet." If you'd just like to view the resources for Chapter 5, you can go to: http://www.delicious.com/brocansky/bptet+ch5. If you'd like to view an interactive wordcloud of all my Delicious tags (click on any tag to view its related sites), go to: http://www.delicious.com/brocansky/tags. What you won't be able to see are the tags I've opted to keep private. For example, if I'm searching for hotels in Mexico for a family vacation and find a site I want to bookmark, I can quickly check the "Mark as Private" box so I am the only one who will see that link in my Delicious links.

Further, Delicious offers the option to curate groups of sites that are referred to as "Stacks." You can build a Stack from the ground up by adding sites one at a time or you can extract bookmarks from those you have already tagged. For example, I pulled all the bookmarks from my account tagged "Twitter" into a Stack titled "Teaching with Twitter." The Stack feature creates a page organized into grids that includes a snippet of the resource in each grid. If the resource is a video, a thumbnail of the video is included in the grid. If there is an image associated with the resource, then the image appears along with the title. The result is a visually pleasing, magazine-like layout of the web resources that are accessible via a single link. To view a Stack of my Teaching with Twitter resources, follow this link: http://www.delicious.com/stacks/view/CpZbRG.

Creating a Stack could be a great group project for a class. Students in a biology class, for example, could be organized into groups of 3–4 students and each group could sign up for a topic from a list shared by their professor. Over the course of a month or so, the students would independently research the topic and evaluate articles, websites, videos, and images against criteria provided by their professor. The criteria may specify that the final Stack must include two videos that feature interviews or presentations of topic experts, four images that illustrate the topic, one general informational resource, and one resource that offers a controversial viewpoint. The students could proceed with collecting their resources by using their individual Delicious accounts and tagging each site they find with a pre-determined tag (that preferably is not used by others). For example, the students may use the course number followed by their topic: bio124cloning. As they independently tag sites with "bio124cloning," anyone could go to delicious.com, enter that tag into the search field and locate all the sites that are associated with it. This way, the students can regularly check in on what their groupmates are tagging and begin to prepare for a final edit to determine which sites will be cut and which sites will be included in the Stack they will submit for their project.

When they're ready, it's simply a manner of designating one student to create the Stack and select the sites they've selected from the "bio124cloning" group of tags. Then the student simply gives the stack a title and a description and, voila, the link is ready to be copied, pasted, and submitted to the professor.

After the sites are evaluated by the professor, they can be shared with the class (again using Delicious!), and students in the class can begin to access, analyze, and discuss the content the students have curated. This could then be followed up with a required blog post in which students write a 500-word summary of what they learned about a new topic from one of the Stacks in the class. After the blogs are finished, the students would then read each others' blogs and engage in a dialogue about the blog posts by leaving comments on each others' posts.

Social bookmarking tools are invaluable for managing the deluge of web-based content we confront each day and the option to share bookmarks with others offers a multitude of teaching and learning possibilities.

Diigo

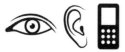   http://www.diigo.com

Feature Overview

- Free social bookmarking tool with premium options.
- Annotate webpages with a highlighter or add sticky notes and archive your customized version for later.

- Search your links and your annotations.
- Use sticky notes on a page to collaborate with other users.
- Extract and compile the content you've highlighted.
- Create private or public groups for easy sharing in a class.
- Mobile app available.

Diigo is a social bookmarking tool that includes features similar to Delicious but extends users the ability to archive customized versions of a webpage by adding their own sticky notes and highlights.

Derek Bruff, referenced earlier in this chapter, requires his statistics students at Vanderbilt University to use Diigo or Pinterest (discussed later in this chapter), to identify and examine real-world applications of data visualization and data analysis that reach outside the boundaries of the curriculum covered in his course. Bruff explains to his students that there are three outcomes of the social bookmarking activity:

1. *To help you make connections between the content of this course and other interests of yours, both academic and personal.*
2. *To enrich the learning experience for all of us (including me) in the class.*
3. *Later in the semester, you'll be asked to complete an application project in which you apply the statistical techniques from this course to some "real world" problem. The collection of examples the class generates through social bookmarking will provide you with lots of potential topics for this project.*[13]

After explaining *how* the tool will enhance the students' learning experience, Bruff gives students an opportunity to evaluate both Diigo and Pinterest and select the tool they prefer. Then he introduces students to the bookmarking process and begins to give assignments to the class requiring them to use the tool of their choice with clear instructions about how to tag the bookmarks in both tools. The first bookmarking assignment he gives is:

- *Find and bookmark an example of data visualization. The more complex the data, the better.*
- *For Diigo users, tag your bookmark with "dataviz." For Pinterest users, include the hashtag "#dataviz" in your bookmark's description.*

By scaffolding the students' exposure to and use of a new tool, openly sharing outcomes, and including himself in the learning community, Bruff demonstrates an effective integration of an emerging technology that is driven by pedagogy. The collections generated by the students are shared with the class, empowering students to become the creators of the course content from which they learn.

BagTheWeb

http://www.bagtheweb.com

Feature Overview

- Create a free, customized list or "bag" of links.
- A simple, no frills method of creating a list or "bag" of links and sharing them with a URL.
- Bags can be private or public.
- Mobile bookmarklet is available. (A bookmarklet is a link within your browser that you click on to add a site to your account.)

BagTheWeb is basic and simple—and that might be just why you like it! Some other content curation tools covered in the following pages offer dynamic, visual layouts that are certainly appealing but sometimes you just want to have a tool that does the basics and that's just what BagTheWeb provides. The simplicity of it makes it a great option for student use, as there's really no training necessary.

When I host a webinar (a live, web-based presentation shared with a group of virtual audience members), I use BagTheWeb to create a list of web-based resources that support my presentation. I share the link to the "Bag" with the participants, coining it their "Goody Bag." Before the webinar I can add all the sites I refer to in my presentation and even go back to the Bag and add more links later if new resources are identified. Using the tool is as simple as creating an account, creating a Bag and clicking on the Add a Link option. Give the link a custom title (the way it will appear in your Bag) and add a brief description. Then keep going until you're done and publish your work or keep it private—it's up to you. You have the option to upload a simple image to differentiate your Bags from one another but other than that, we've covered the basics.

TIP

Use the BagTheWeb widget to embed a bag of links on your website, blog, or course management system . . . or have your students do the same to share the course-related resources they've collected!

Scoop.it

 http://www.scoop.it

Feature Overview

- Select a topic and collect links about that topic, arranged in a visual online magazine format.
- Free tool with premium options.
- Make curation collaborative by granting permission to other users to add posts to your topic.
- Leave comments on any item in a topic.
- Auto-share to social media tools (for example, your Facebook or Twitter account).
- Mobile app available for iPhone and iPad.

Scoop.it is a site that can be used to create a magazine-like collection of web resources that support any given topic. You can also use Scoop.it to follow topics curated by other users. After selecting your topic, you will be able to review suggested resources via the dashboard page in Scoop.it. The suggested resources are mined from sources that you can customize (for example, you can add a Twitter user who is an expert on the topic or delete any of the sources Scoop.it has recommended). As topics are suggested, you select which ones you want to add as posts within your topic.

With a free account, a user can curate up to five collections and this number increases if you upgrade to one of the premium account options. And, as the lead creator of a Scoop.it topic, you can add emails of additional users who you'd like to be able to add posts to your collection.

TIP

Use the Bookmarklet for Fast and Easy Curation!

As you begin to get your arms around using Scoop.it or any other content curation tool, the quality of your experience as well as your content will improve by using the tool's bookmarklet. A bookmarklet is a tiny little application that you can simply drag and drop into the top of your browser (in the bookmark bar). Once it's installed there, you can click on it to seamlessly add a webpage you are on to the collection you're curating with that specific tool. Diigo, Delicious, and Pinterest also have bookmarklets.

Pinterest

 www.pinterest.com

Feature Overview

- Free tool.
- Pin icons of websites to a bulletin-board-like interface.
- Re-pin items shared by other users.
- Follow boards made by other users.
- Leave comments on any pinned item.
- You decide who can pin to each of your boards—just you or other Pinterest account holders who you follow.
- Mobile app available for iPhone, allowing users to pin images to a board that they've taken with their phone.

Pinterest is a tool that has picked up a lot of followers. Its ease of use and visually appealing interface make it a fun tool to use. Once you've installed the bookmarklet (see Tip above), pinning is easy. Just click the "Pin This" icon that sits within your browser's toolbar and a window pops up asking you to identify which of your boards you'd like to pin the site to. I am using Pinterest with my History of Photography students as a way for me to provide them with an array of images for writing their blog posts. In the past, I used to point them to external websites that provide public access to photographic collections. That was tricky because it always required students to

Figure 5.7 Pinterest screenshot. Used with permission from Pinterest.

navigate the databases and I risked having them select an image that didn't fit within the criteria for the assignment. So now I am generating boards on Pinterest that include collections of specific types of images (19th-century post mortem daguerreotypes, spirit photography, etc.).

Pinterest is a social tool and, like all social media, its fullest potential is felt when users engage each others' boards, re-pin, and comment on the sites. I haven't yet worked Pinterest into my class in a social way but I'm working on it. One thing that would make this process easier for professors would be if there were a method of inviting collaborators to a board through an invitation link or a special "code." Unfortunately, the only way to add collaborators to one of your boards is to follow one of their boards and then select their name from a list. For now, this process is tricky when working with large groups of students. But if you teach a visually oriented class, check out Pinterest—you'll find a way to make it work!

The mobile app adds an intriguing dimension to "pinning," as you could require your students to take photographs during a field trip or on an independent quest to locate particular specimens of flowers or other course-related content and then students could use the app to pin the images to a board (within their own Pinterest account). Students could then paste the links to their Pinterest boards within your course (a great use for a collaborative Google Doc!) and then students could click on the links, follow each others' boards, and leave comments on the images.

Assessing Participatory Learning

Identifying a plan for grading the work that students contribute in response to participatory learning activities can be baffling at first. The key is to step back and don't let the digital format of their work throw you for a loop. Just because there isn't a tangible stack of papers in front of you to grade, doesn't mean there isn't evidence of learning. Instead, as you develop an activity (or a series of activities for a course), keep an eye on what the learning outcomes are. More specifically, identify exactly what the students are 1) required to do and 2) how their contributions will demonstrate that they've learned. Then organize this information into a rubric and share the rubric with students prior to the initiation of the activity or project.

To help you get started with creating rubrics for participatory, digital learning activities, you may find it helpful to view some samples. The Eberly Center for Teaching and Learning at Carnegie Mellon shares many fine examples of rubrics for a variety of projects and activities for different disciplines (http://www.cmu.edu/teaching/assessment/examples/courselevel-bycollege/index.html). According to the Eberly Center, a rubric should contain:

- Criteria: the aspects of performance (e.g., argument, evidence, clarity) that will be assessed.
- Descriptors: the characteristics associated with each dimension (e.g., argument is demonstrable and original, evidence is diverse and compelling).
- Performance levels: a rating scale that identifies students' level of mastery within each criterion.

The sample rubric shared below in Figure 5.8 is one that I use to assess VoiceThreads in my online class that I use as general formative assessments. In these activities, students listen to my instructions, view a mini video lecture/presentation, and respond to prompts I have written. They receive up to 10 points for their contributions and they are graded on three criteria: originality, comprehension, and clarity.

The Role of Social Media in the Future of College Learning

How will social media reshape the future of college learning? That's an exciting question to ponder and in the case studies included in this chapter, we can see some glimpses into the future. It is likely that we will continue to see more professors who steer away from textbooks for providing course content and experiment more with connecting students to user-generated content in an effort to engage them in a critical inquiry about particular topics or problems.

Jason Rosenblum, an educational technologist at St. Edward's University, takes an intriguing approach to teaching his Global Social Problems course—and I think it serves as a nice example of a forward-thinking teaching model. Together with Robert Strong, an associate professor in University Programs at St. Edward's, these instructors take a gameful approach by challenging students to complete a series of three missions—to Research global social problems, take Action (online and face-to-face) to deal with those problems, and finally to Imagine potential solutions with those problems to successfully complete the course. As Rosenblum points out:

> Our course was heavily inspired by the work of Jane McGonigal (http://jane mcgonigal.com/) and her work to inspire gameful participation to deal with real-life social issues in her alternate realty game (ARG), Evoke (http://www.urgent evoke.com/). We wanted to challenge people to take Heroic action to deal with serious global social problems. We incorporated social media in significant ways in the course; first, as a tool for research and second as a tool to take action to deal with their chosen problem. Students used social media tools such as Twitter, Facebook, Mashable, Evri and Scoop.it to research and take action to deal with problems that included water security, gender inequality, poverty, and the war in the Democratic Republic of the Congo. Students even participated in the live stream of the Social Good Summit, an event that highlighted the importance of using technology such as social media, for social good (http://mashable.com/sgs/). All course participation was public on the course site, and students were required to write blog posts and reflections based on their research and social media activities. Our goal was to design a class in which course participation was grounded in a set of Heroic Character Traits (e.g. tenacity, courage, empathy, credibility, etc.), and in which the assessment for every course activity was relevant and authentic.

In Rosenblum and Strong's model, students learn how to locate pertinent information, examine the conversations, and think critically about them. Examples of this

	Exemplary - 3.33	Developing - 2	Beginning - 1	No Credit - 0
Originality	The minimum number of comments are left and all comments are in the student's own words and contribute unique viewpoints or ideas.	Comment(s) are in the student's own words and contribute mostly unique viewpoints or ideas.	Student comment(s) demonstrate repetition of ideas contributed in previous comments.	Student comment(s) demonstrate evidence of plagiarism.
Comprehension	The minimum number of comments are left and all comments demonstrate an understanding of the related concepts and ideas and may demonstrate an effort to build on previous students comments left on the slide.	Comment(s) demonstrate an attempt to understand the related concepts and ideas.	Comment(s) demonstrate little to no understanding of the related concepts and ideas.	Student comment(s) demonstrate evidence of plagiarism.
Clarity	The minimum number of comments are left and all comments are clear and understandable.	Written or spoken comments are mostly clear and understandable.	Written or spoken comments are not clear or understandable.	Student comment(s) demonstrate evidence of plagiarism.

Figure 5.8 Rubric sample.

can be found through social media activities in the Action mission, where students were asked to locate articles online which were pertinent to their chosen global social issues. Students then needed to post a comment to those articles and write a blog entry that demonstrated a reflection of their process to critically evaluate and respond to these articles online. In one instance, a student chose to respond to an article about birth control on the New York Times' website comment area. This student's comment was not only subsequently "recommended" by over 40 other readers, the Times decided to promote the comment by making it one of a smaller number of "Highlighted" comments on a popular Times article.

Successful completion of the missions in the course was evaluated through a series of rubrics that emphasized students' ability to critically analyze and synthesize material from research and activities that involved not only traditional academic sources, but also social media sources including Facebook, Twitter and a variety of other online socially-enabled content. All course outcomes were designed to be authentic. According to Rosenblum:

> As educators we should inquire—early and often—what it means for students to live and learn in a globally-connected world. How can we help students to develop the critical literacies they need to not only consume content, but also create knowledge?

These learning outcomes are, arguably, essential 21st-century literacies for students living in a mobile, digital world. As they embark on their missions, students become active participants in existing online conversations about a topic of their choice and are also empowered to begin and lead new conversations. Their quest is to change the world—quite a lofty objective for a college course, I'd say.

Rosenblum and Strong's course policy webpage explains how their students are expected to use social media in the class. (You may view the webpage at: http://academic.stedwards.edu/globalsocialproblems/page/policies or access it in the Chapter 5 resources.) Students are required to connect their Twitter account to the course website and to tweet their blog postings using the course hashtag, #globsoc. In addition, students are strongly encouraged to use Twitter for research and to share information relevant to their topics through Tweets and re-Tweets, finding and following Twitter users who share content related to their topic, creating lists to organize content, and sharing other course-related content with the #globsoc hashtag. Students are also encouraged to use Facebook to research the activities of non-profit organizations and other users that are relevant to their selected topic. The course policy webpage includes best practices and information about university policies. Expectations are clearly communicated upfront—an essential part of teaching effectively with emerging technologies. And, what of the student experience? The course instructors provided one quote by a student describing their overall course experience.

> *I got a lot out of this course. I have always been a very passionate person with anything that I've ever set my mind to, whether it be my career in the arts or my school work. This class*

was a wonderful way to make people really work to change the world, and not just to write one more paper on it. I was able to reach out and actually change lives in this course and that is amazing.

All in all, this approach to learning empowers students to become actively involved with real-world scenarios and learn that they really can make a difference. Through their participation through Twitter, Facebook and other social media tools they learn, through experience, the power that social media holds for giving each member of our society a voice. They learn how their participation in social media can contribute to changing the world, as opposed to using it to inform the world about what they had for dinner.

Summary

Building off the momentum we established in Chapter 4, this chapter has augmented your teaching toolkit to include an array of social technologies, many of which are supported with mobile apps, that offer options for creating student-centered learning activities. The tools here are merely colors in a palette. Like an artist, your task is to select a tool and align it with your own creative vision to construct relevant, engaging learning activities for your students.

In Chapter 6, we will build upon our momentum further by maintaining a focus on collaborative, participatory learning but shifting the emphasis to mobility. Chapter 6 examines the significance of mobile learning on 21st-century higher education and asks whether "mobile learning is smarter learning?"

Chapter 6

Mobile and Beyond

Mobile learning is a thread woven throughout this entire book. In the introduction, I shared my 2009 "flipped classroom" experiment in which students had the option to listen to lectures on a computer or opt for a mobile learning experience by listening to them on the go from an iPod or other supported mobile device. Also, within the introductory chapter, we considered the ways that mobile learning supports some of the key tenets of brain research. In Chapter 1, we discussed the importance of including in your syllabus a clear listing of mobile apps that could be used by students in your class to ensure students start off on the right foot. In Chapter 2, we considered how mobile devices are altering the way students learn and identified mobile support as one of the elements of evaluating a tool's accessibility. And in Chapters 3, 4, and 5 we examined a collection of tools and highlighted those that are available in the form of a mobile app (an item you will most definitely want to check on for yourself, as mobile app development is moving at lightning speed).

In this chapter, we veer away from specific apps and consider mobility in a new dimension. This chapter offers a deeper exploration into the mainstream adoption of internet-connected mobile devices and encourages you to consider many of the ways they may impact your teaching and the possibilities they hold for reinventing your students' learning.

The term "mobile learning" refers to learning that occurs through the use of a handheld mobile device. There are many types of mobile devices ranging from handheld video cameras to PDAs, iPods, feature phones, smartphones, and tablet PCs. This chapter will focus on smartphones and tablet PCs, specifically the iPad, as these internet connected, handheld computers are the fastest growing segment of mobile devices and are poised to make the greatest splash in the future of higher education. In fact, mobile apps (the applications that run on smartphones and iPads) and tablets were showcased front and center in the 2012 Horizon Report, an annual report by the New Media Consortium that traces the pulse of emerging technologies making waves in the near future.[1] This chapter does not attempt to define how mobility will change the world or formalized learning but it will illuminate some of the trends and pose some provocative questions about the road ahead.

Mobile Devices: Faculty Foe or Friend?

In 2009, I attended my first conference about "mobile learning" at Pasadena City College. The keynote presentation was given by a group of representatives from Abilene Christian University (ACU), an institution that was unfamiliar to me at that time. Bill Rankin, a red-haired medievalist-turned-education-technology-innovator, paced thoughtfully beneath a dazzling presentation that showcased captivating images of the iPhone and iPod Touch, two handheld "mobile" communication devices that connect a user to the internet; can take photographs and videos; run an array of free to low-cost apps, each adding a unique functionality; and, in the case of the iPhone, send and receive text messages and phone calls.

While most professors were (and many still are) scratching their heads about how to keep these disruptive devices *out* of their classrooms, Rankin announced that ACU had begun to give one to all their incoming freshmen students. *Gulp.* What did the students at ACU need to do in exchange for the device? They had to agree to bring it to campus and use it in class. No, this was not a deceptive ploy to agitate professors enough to trigger a large-scale early retirement. Rather, it was an experiment driven by the question, "When we can hold a universe of information in the palms of our hands, how does that change the way we learn and communicate?"[2] In fact, an important component of the mobile initiative (and should be for *any* mobile initiative) was having professors take workshops designed to help them understand how to use the devices, *as well as* how to use them in class to best support student learning. At ACU, undergraduate teaching is a *practice* and practice involves making mistakes, pushing the limits, being propelled by inquiry—*practice is perpetual learning*.

Also at the heart of ACU's mobile initiative—which is now internationally acclaimed and has been rebranded as ACU Connected, and has received funding from a host of external sources including AT&T and Next Generation Learning Challenge—is the vision that "humans learn best when they are in community—collaborating with others in a learning environment without boundaries."[3] While mobile devices are often envisioned merely as a gateway to information; ACU realized early on that they hold great potential for connecting students with their peers and other users around the world, resulting in an increased exchange of ideas, exposure to new ways of understanding old problems, and an invitation to contribute to a growing global discourse. But the success of this vision depended on ubiquitous access, to ensure all students could be included in the practice.

TIP

Feature Phones, Smartphones, Tablets, Oh My!

The simple chart in Figure 6.1 explains the typical features of the three most popular mobile devices.

	Voice	Text Messaging	Internet*	Apps	Still Camera	Video Camera
Feature Phone	✓	✓			✓	varies
Smartphone (iPhone, Droid, MyTouch)	✓	✓	✓	✓	✓	✓
Tablet PC (iPad, Xoom, Galaxy)			✓	✓	✓	✓

Figure 6.1 Mobile device chart.

*Smartphones and tablet PCs have two methods of connecting to the internet: cellular transmission (3G, 4G) which is the same type of connection feature phones rely on for voice and text communications and/or wireless (WiFi). If a student is in a classroom with a WiFi device, connecting to the internet is only possible if the institution provides WiFi network access to students.

Mobile Goes Mainstream

Since the inauguration of the iPhone in 2007, the smartphone market has changed quite a bit and while most college classrooms may not have reached ubiquitous access, we are moving downstream . . . swiftly. Early on, the iPhone's stiff price point and hefty monthly charge for the mandatory data plan positioned it as a luxury item that most of us longed for. But the next year, the playing field began to shift when Google released the Android mobile operating system, resulting in a blossoming of new smartphones on the market. In the years that followed, increased competition lowered the price point for smartphones and in March 2012, a survey conducted by the Pew Internet & American Life Project revealed that nerly half of American adults (46%) own a smartphone.[4] And a survey from Ericsson forecasts that by 2015, 80% of all people accessing the internet will do so from a mobile device.[5]

While smartphones were once considered a way of extending internet access beyond the walls of home and office, they are now being used for very different purposes by some groups of users. According to Pew, in 2011 the three groups most likely to purchase a smartphone in the United States were the financially well-off (59%), followed by those with a college degree (48%), and a close third were African Americans and Latinos (44%). Now let's peel this data back one more layer. Smartphone owners who are non–white and under age 30, according to the Pew survey, who also have a relatively low income and education level are those who are *most likely* to use their mobile device to access the internet—meaning their smartphone *is their internet access.*

Why is this so important to college educators? Well, I teach at a community college and interact with many community college instructors about the possibilities of using social media and mobile learning in college classes. I commonly hear instructors say, "I can't do that because my students can't afford smartphones." I carry that comment with me all the time and think about it when I read these statistics. While I don't advocate assuming all students have access to *any* technology, I am concerned that college educators are disconnected from the realities of smartphone ownership.

To some people, smartphones are convenient "add-ons" to a home landline and broadband access. But this is changing—*quickly*. Everyday, more and more people (many of them traditional college-age) are foregoing the option to pay for a landline, home broadband access and television and instead, purchase one or more smartphones within their family for handheld, bundled access to voice, text, internet and media (for less than 10 dollars a month a smartphone user can watch all the movies and available TV episodes they want with the free NetFlix app!)

Viewing a smartphone as a luxury item available only to those with disposable income is problematic because it affects the way we, as educators, relate to and value these devices and, in turn, informs our behaviors about using them in our classes. In 2011, I attended a session at a conference in which the presenter showcased a new tool that students could access from a laptop in class. I raised my hand and inquired about whether or not the tool was available also in the form of a mobile app (which would enable students who have a smartphone but no laptop to use it—as we'll soon discuss, not *all* web-based content is viewable on *all* mobiles). The presenter replied, "No, we haven't developed a mobile app because we assume if students can afford a smartphone, then they're already going to have a laptop." I shook my head.

All college stakeholders—regardless of your institutional role—need to comprehend the sweeping impact of mobile devices in 21st-century life and understand how they are changing the way information is accessed; changing the user experience; and creating a flatter, more collaborative global society. More specifically, it's imperative to understand that the experience of accessing information on a smartphone is unique from accessing the same content on a laptop or desktop. (Go ahead—try it! Log into your class from a computer and then try to do so from a smartphone. Have fun with that.) Some websites, for example, do not even load on a mobile device, others include content (like Flash) that doesn't render on some mobile devices, and others load but trying to click on the tiny links on a three-inch screen to navigate through the necessary pages feels like threading a needle.

Considering the mobile user experience also adds layers of complexity to course design and new considerations for all web-based student services. But thinking inclusively about mobility also activates new paradigms for how we communicate with students, how and where they access their learning content, and unravels our traditional expectations about college assessment too.

It's important for 21st-century higher ed institutions to recognize and understand these nuances to make mobile users a priority. Moreover, a consistent institutional effort to track and communicate the percentage of enrolled students who have a smartphone and/or a tablet PC would be of tremendous value to professors. This data would allow instructors to make decisions about integrating mobile learning into their classes within a culture of evidence, rather than a fog of assumptions.

Preparing Students for the Real World

One winter day in 2012, I was driving into downtown Sacramento for a business meeting. I was meeting at an office that I had not been to before. All I had was an address, a name, and an understanding that the person I would be meeting with was an executive within a multi-million dollar company. When I arrived at the office building, I didn't find the traditional, well-manicured office space that I expected to represent a large, flourishing company. Rather, I walked right into the Urban Hive, an industrial warehouse located next to a train track in the heart of Sacramento. The building exudes energy. The interior is organized into flexible workspaces, referred to as "un-offices," that promote collaboration and multitasking. There is a large group room for multiple people to work from laptops or tablets alongside one another, a few private offices available for lease, conference rooms for spontaneous gatherings, an art gallery, a beer tap and a small store that sells record albums from the '60s and '70s. Eclectic, creative, contemporary—and mobile.

The Urban Hive is a 21st-century office space from which multi-million dollar companies are run and young entrepreneurs put their ideas into action when they aren't on a plane. In the end, it is a collaborative community of people whose careers thrive on a constant flow of new ideas. As you look around the Urban Hive, you see dedicated, talented, focused individuals who rely upon being mobile to be effective at what they do. Urban Hive is the workplace of the future.

Mobility is reshaping the way people work. Each year, it becomes less and less likely that future generations will be commuting to an office (or at least the same office) every-day. According to projections from the Market Intelligence firm, IDC, one third of the global workforce, or 1.2 billion workers, will work from multiple locations by 2013.[6]

After college, students who enter a corporate environment will more than likely engage in mobile learning as a form of training or professional development. According to a 2011 survey conducted by the American Society of Training and Development (ASTD) and the Institute for Corporate Productivity (i4cp), 85% of companies provide mobile devices to at least some of their workforce. Moreover, 15% of the companies surveyed already have a mobile learning initiative in place for their employees' training and 60% are either considering it or already developing one.[7]

Mobile devices are at the core of this workforce transformation and encouraging students to learn how to use them to foster collaboration, is an important step in preparing students for success in the 21st century. As such, "mobile literacy" is a growing area of scholarship and students at universities around the world are currently preparing for careers in mobile application development. As David Parry, assistant professor of emerging media and communications at the University of Texas at Dallas, argues, "The future our students will inherit is one that will be mediated and stitched together by the mobile web, and I think that ethically, we are called on as teachers to teach them how to use these technologies effectively."[8]

Getting Started: Setting the Norms

Figure 6.2
No cell phones.
Photo by
Michael Derr,
used with
permission.

In March 2010, EDUCAUSE held a two-day online summit about mobile learning in higher education. One of the presenters shared a story that offers an intriguing metaphor for the topic. The story described the strategies employed by the people in two Chinese villages in preparation for the increased water run off from melted snow in the spring. One village employed the strategy to build dams to ward the water off and keep it out of their village. The other accepted that the water was on its way and worked together to dig channels throughout the village so the water could continue to flow through the village without causing damage.

In many ways, that metaphor offers two very different strategies for negotiating our students' use of mobile devices in the classroom. Smartphones are part of our students' culture. They hold a significant place in the lives of most college students and, as such, inform their behaviors, their preferences, and their values. In various chapters of this book, we've discussed the importance of fostering community in a class, starting with day one, to establish the foundation of a successful participatory learning environment. A community is a group of individuals working together—leaning on one another, giving to and taking from one another—to meet a common goal. When a student walks into a classroom and sees a sign that says "No Cell Phone Use," it can create a sense of isolation, leaving students feeling disconnected and marginalized, rather than engaged and included. These attitudes work to create problematic barriers that situate "them" and "us" in different camps and undermine the goal of working together, learning together, in community.

You don't need to be part of a campus-wide mobile initiative to explore the benefits of mobility in your students' learning (but nobody would disagree that it would be fabulous if we all had access to such fantastic projects!). This book has included an array of examples of how college professors—full-time and part-time, from public and private, as well as two-year and four-year institutions—are weaving smartphones or mobile apps into their students' learning. When students understand that you view a phone as a learning tool, they will relate to you and your class differently. It sets a norm in a class and demonstrates that you accept and understand your students' world. It's a gesture that signifies your acceptance of their culture.

This doesn't mean you are granting your students free reign to chat, text, make phone calls, check Facebook, or book their plane ticket for their upcoming Vegas trip in your class. As discussed in Chapter 1, establishing a set of community groundrules at the start of the term is your opportunity to set the norms that you and your students will model week after week. So, rather than "no cell phones," maybe what we should be saying is, "In this class, you will be invited to use your phone for a variety of learning activities. If you need to use your phone for a reason that does not support your learning, please excuse yourself from the classroom."

When your class is designed to ensure students will spend class time actively constructing knowledge, learning in community with their peers, engaged in activities that embrace tools they use everyday outside of class, they're going to be present. So, start digging those channels and let the water flow. . .

Designing for Multiple Screens

"Know who your students are" is a key principle in designing and facilitating an online course. From an operating systems' perspective, we used to think about meeting the needs of both PC and Mac users but now we need to be conscious about mobile operating systems too—yikes! Here are some of the things you should think about as you prepare to use smartphones in your traditional classroom, as a learning enhancement between classes, or in support of online learning.

Which Activities Are Appropriate for Mobile?

You aren't going to want all of your students' work generated from a smartphone. Clearly some activities are more appropriate for mobile use than others. Which are they?

For example, I regularly require my students to write 500-word reflective blog posts in response to a carefully constructed prompt. A three-inch screen with a handheld keyboard probably isn't the best method for developing a well thought out, grammatically correct, spelling-error-free, reflective writing assignment. But other activities make good sense for mobile—and if you don't have any that do, that's a perfect starting point for integrating mobile learning!

As discussed in Chapter 3, it's important to include mobile support as one of your criteria for evaluating new tools in your class. And if you're already using particular emerging technologies, it's a good idea, before your next term starts, to do a tool check-in and identify if the tools are now available in a mobile app (and on which iOS platforms-for example, Android and Apple iOS? Apple iOS is the operating system that runs on all Apple mobile devices: iPhones, iPads and iPod Touches). This could be as simple as doing a web search for the tool and checking the website (mobile apps are commonly listed in a section titled "Tools") or contacting your institution's academic technology or instructional technology staff, who may be able to provide you with some valuable information about the mobile app. If you do this check-in on your own, it's advisable that you download the mobile app onto your own smartphone, if you have one, or read about the app's features on the website (you may also try searching the web for some user reviews of the app). This step will help you identify how the mobile app differs in functionality from the web application, which is important information to include when sharing it with your students.

To inform your students about the option to use a tool in mobile app form, make a note in your syllabus and course assignments to indicate when an activity supports mobile. Consider using a small icon to designate "mobile worthy" activities. Your students will appreciate your efforts to make their everyday tools part of their college learning experience and your clear instructions will add flexibility and convenience to their college learning experience.

Integrating Mobile Apps

The 2012 Horizon Report, an annual document from the New Media Consortium that showcases emerging technologies poised to make the most impact on higher education over the next several years, featured mobile apps front and center. Mobile apps, to review, are applications designed to run specifically on a mobile operating system—which could be on a smartphone or on a tablet. And remember, each app may be available for just one operating system or for several. These are moving targets, as developers of web-based applications (like those featured in this book) are racing to develop apps for a range of mobile operating systems. In 2009 there were about 35,000 apps available in the Apple App Store. At the start of 2012, there were nearly 600,000.[9]

Visiting an app store online is like a virtual visit to a candy store—the brilliant colored app logos are mesmerizing and tempt you with their free to low-cost price tags. Apps are focused on delivering a specific functionality—creating a video, editing an image, showcasing 3-D models of molecules, or mapping a real time view of the stars above as you walk through a campground. Whatever your discipline is, you'll find something to suit you!

A smartphone or tablet can easily be customized with a suite of apps to support a specific course or discipline at a lower cost than a complete software set up for a desktop computer. Apps have reinvented software. But most of us do not teach to a group of students who all have access to the same mobile device—so the integration of apps into a class needs to be done with a careful consideration of your audience.

As I mentioned above, writing a blog post is an activity that is better suited for a computer than a mobile device and in education, we are more comfortable with giving writing and reading assignments. But when many of our students have the equivalent of a multimedia lab in their pocket, new options surface for diversifying activities beyond reading and writing.

For example, you could require students to take photographs that demonstrate a particular concept or idea from your curriculum and have them share those images with the class immediately, rather than needing to wait until they get back to a computer to download an image from a digital camera. When a camera is in your pocket *at all times*, you have more opportunities to document your visual surroundings (or share fleeting questions and reflections via Twitter!). Just-in-time sharing means students will be more likely to complete activities earlier in a unit, allowing more time for side discussions to develop.

TIP

Easy (Mobile) Group Blogging With Posterous!

If you like the idea of having students take and share images (or videos for that matter) but are stumped about how to facilitate the sharing of the media within your class, check out Posterous.com. Posterous is a blogging platform (with a mobile app) that gives you the option to create a blog by a single user or a group blog.

With the group blog feature you can grant publishing privileges to all the students in your class. But, wait! It gets better. The best part about Posterous is that each blog comes along with a unique email address. Anything that is sent to that email address gets processed and published as a new blog post!

Display the link to the Posterous group blog within your course management system (or create a button in the navigation menu that links out to the blog) and encourage students to view and comment on each others' work, as the entries are submitted via email directly to the blog! The student-generated content could also be leveraged as topics for discussion posts, papers, or even essay questions for exams.

Here is a specific example of how mobile learning has affected my online teaching approach. I use VoiceThread (discussed in the Introduction and Chapters 4 and 5) in my online classes and I have been eager to get more students to leave voice comments. I have found that most students resort to leaving text comments because of many reasons—it's what they're used to and it's just faster—despite the fact that at the end of each term, most students share that they wish more students had used voice comments! From surveys, I knew there were some students in my classes who didn't have access to a microphone or webcam and I didn't like the idea of requiring online students to come to campus to use these tools. I was also aware that many students are reluctant to comment in voice and video because they feel intimidated and fear that they will "sound stupid." But, to me, communicating verbally is an important part of a college learning experience and that's one of the reasons I am striving to make student-generated voice or video comments integral to all of my online classes.

This problem started to shift for me in Fall of 2011, when VoiceThread released a free mobile app that allows a user to leave comments in voice or video from an iPhone or iPad. I surveyed my students at the start of the next term to identify if they had a method for leaving a voice or video comment. Thirty-three percent of students said they had a microphone, 30% had a webcam, and 30% *had an iPhone or iPad*. That left only 7% (2 students) who needed assistance with gaining access to a commenting method (which I provided by adding additional phone commenting minutes to their VoiceThread account a feature available to users with a department account or site license to VoiceThread).

This example demonstrates how the integration of mobile apps into your class puts multimedia creation tools into the hands of more of your students. As a result, your options for how you assess student learning have blossomed into activities that integrate audio, video, and image creation.

Designing for multiple screens is a topic that extends well beyond the considerations of just faculty and instructional designers. Each year, more and more institutions of higher ed embrace mobile as a priority in the development of their web services. First steps involve integrating a website that is optimized for mobile devices. This improves a user's experience by displaying a site on a mobile screen that is designed to be easily viewed and navigated from a small screen.

Beyond websites optimized for mobile viewing, many institutions have teams focused on the development of apps for a range of student uses. The forward-thinking team in the Rosen Center for Advanced Computing at Purdue University has harnessed the power and possibilities of mobile learning, cloud computing, and social media in an impressive application called Mixable. Mixable is available for students to use from either a computer or mobile app and was developed to empower students to manage their own learning with tools that are familiar to them. Professors at Purdue use a course management system to organize and share content with students, and students can use Mixable to add a social layer to their learning.

Kyle Bowen, director of informatics and project lead for Mixable, explains, "Courses in Blackboard are typically delivered in a top-down fashion, where the faculty drive most activities. In contrast, Mixable grants students control of the conversation. Mixable also allows students to share their resources and discussions across courses—something that can be difficult to do with current systems."[10]

Mixable recontextualizes a students' learning within the social media tools they already use. For example, students can engage in a discussion about a course in Facebook or Twitter and Mixable will provide Facebook friend suggestions based upon course enrollment information. Students can easily share links to online articles and when visual content like images or videos is shared, a small thumbnail version of the content is embedded within the post.

Also appealing is the integration of Mixable with Echo360, a premium lecture caption system in use across campus. When a professor shares a lecture with his students using Echo360, the students automatically have the option to view and listen to it on the go using Mixable, rather than needing to launch a browser on their smartphone

Figure 6.4 Mixable app. Used with permission from Purdue University.

Figure 6.5 OSU app. Used with permission from Ohio State University.

and struggle through a maze of clicks to locate and play the file. Finally, students can use Mixable as a mobile Flash drive because it is integrated with Dropbox (discussed in Chapter 3), a cloud-based file hosting application. For more about Mixable, go to: http://www.itap.purdue.edu/studio/mixable/.

Ohio State is one of the many colleges and universities who have developed a mobile app for students. After downloading the free app, students can use it to view grades, check the real-time bus schedule, connect to OSU's Facebook page and Twitter feed, access lectures on iTunes U, get walking directions to any destination on campus, see a list of restaurants nearby, search the library's catalog, view the current balance in their student account, or peruse the class schedule. If students don't have a smartphone, they can access the same resources through the university's mobile website at: http://m.osu.edu.

Is Mobile Learning *Smarter* Learning?

If your brain learns more effectively while you are active, as brain researchers claim, mobile devices may have a silver lining that has yet to be realized.[11] According to a Dutch study from 2012, there is evidence that there is a correlation between increased physical activity and better grades in school children.[12]

Videos and audio files can be downloaded or viewed online with a single tap on a smartphone, providing the option to blend a class lecture into the mix of everyday life. And creating a video lecture is now as simple as recording direct from your webcam into your free YouTube account and sharing the link with your students. How will these emerging trends impact the future of higher education?

But learning on the go doesn't just change how we learn, it may change *what* we learn too. I realized this back in 2009 while listening to one of my students reflect about how listening to our lectures while she was cooking dinner or doing laundry wasn't just more convenient but the experience afforded her different ways of thinking about the material. Similarly, another student in that class commented on how listening to a lecture about gender relations while walking across campus, resulted in her applying what she was hearing to her surroundings at that moment. She paused and began to observe the power dynamics between her peers on campus and analyzed how they related to the lecture streaming from her ear buds. Making lectures mobile infuses more than just extra oxygen into our students' bloodstreams. It creates new contexts for learning which may be a pathway to improving critical thinking skills.

Personally, the vision of blending learning into physical activities or even new surroundings feels refreshing to me after so many decades of doom and gloom predictions about our sedentary lifestyle. *Shouldn't this be a topic to rejoice?* Since the popularization of the television in the 1950s, consuming media content has tied us to the couch . . . but no longer. As smartphones continue to go mainstream, learning on the go is a choice for more and more of us.

Get Out of the Classroom: Location, Game-Based Learning

Smartphones and tablets also include their own global positioning software (GPS) which, provided this feature is enabled, allows the apps installed on the device to access the location and push customized content to the user based on her physical location.

Figure 6.6 Dow Day screenshot. Used with permission from Jim Mathews, creator of Dow Day.

Location-based learning is an intriguing way to create game-like activities that set students on an inquiry-based journey through a physical space, blending virtual space with their physical surroundings to produce an experiential learning adventure.

The Dow Day app provides a perfect example. Dow Day is an application authored by Jim Mathews that engages gaming theory to produce learning that is inquiry based, encouraging a learner to take on new identities, solve problems, and even travel back in time. Dow Day falls into the category of "augmented reality" (AR), which is a gaming term for an experience that interlaces digital information with one's real world situation to foster an individualized experience of one's physical environment. As a person walks through his physical environment, an AR application delivers content to a handheld mobile device (video, audio, text, images) that informs how he relates to his environment. AR is not like an audio tour, however. The distinguishing factor is that augmented reality places a user within a problem that must be actively solved by moving through one's environment and critically processing and responding to the information provided.

For example, Dow Day, which was originally designed for a high school curriculum, takes you back in time to 1967 at the University of Wisconsin at Madison. You are challenged to take on the role of a newspaper investigator tasked with investigating breaking details about a series of anti-Vietnam protests that are unfolding across campus.

The game begins by delivering a task to you, via your mobile phone. The text on your screen reads, "Go see your editor." You toggle over to the map on your phone, which is connected to your phone's GPS, and see your location as well as the location of the editor on campus. You begin to walk to meet the editor, following the prompts on your mobile map. When you arrive at the editor's noted location, your phone vibrates and plays a tone. You glance at your phone and see a photograph of the editor who describes what's happening on campus. He gives you a few hints about marchers protesting in one corner of campus and shares that a representative of the Dow Chemical Corporation, which is the company students are protesting, is present in another location. Your task is to follow up on these leads to uncover more details through the historical documents shared with you in the game (documentary videos, news articles, photographs, and graphs). By moving across the campus, you meet individuals with a variety of positions and interests, you ask questions, uncover details, analyze information, and you develop your article. All in all, Dow Day leverages the power of mobile learning and location-based software to challenge users to solve real-life journalistic problems. The learner's outcome is to write a news article that reports on the historical protests, leveraging data from primary sources.

While Dow Day was originally created using a the MITAR platform, developed at MIT, the current version operates on a free, open source mobile platform developed at the University of Wisconsin called ARIS (http://arisgames.org). Even if you aren't on site at the University of Wisconsin at Madison, you can still explore Dow Day at: http://arisgames.org/featured/dow-day by scanning one of the QR Codes on the website (see discussion below) and meet a virtual character or two.

ARIS is a mobile authoring tool that can be used by anyone to develop and play mobile games and create learning experiences with augmented reality. While developing a mobile application probably feels like a stretch for you, it's certainly good to know about ARIS and discuss it with your academic technology support representatives. Who knows, maybe someday you'll have an AR game to share with your students.

QR Codes

Quick Response Codes (better known as QR Codes) are bar codes encrypted with information that can be decoded with an app installed on a mobile device. They're used across an array of industries and are making waves in education too. QR Codes do not necessarily need to correlate with a location-based activity; rather, they could be used to enhance the information made available within a person's physical context. For example, I could distribute a syllabus in my classroom with a QR Code printed on it that, when scanned with a smartphone, would take a student directly to the log-in screen for the course. Or I could place a QR Code on my office door so when a student visits at a time I'm unavailable, the code would launch my contact page on their phone and make it easier to click my phone number to call me, send me an email, or add my info to their contact list.

QR Codes are not limited to containing URLs. They can also be coded with written information (like how the painting in front of you was made), a phone number (scan it and the number is dialed), an SMS text message (that is sent to the phone upon scanning the code), and a vCard (electronic business card). Creating QR Codes is simple. Just choose from one of many, many free tools. I created the one printed here (Figure 6.7) using goqr.me. If you scan it with a QR Code reader app, it will take you directly to the online resource site for this book. Goqr.me is free, provides a range of content options, and allows you to select the resolution of the image you'd like—which is a premium feature of many other QR code generators.

The tricky part about QR Codes is the fact that you need to have a third party QR Code reader app installed on your mobile device in order to scan it and decode its information. This isn't difficult by any means but it's not a concept that is innately understood. There are a variety of free apps available that support the different mobile operating systems. QuickMark (http://www.quickmark.com.tw) is a popular app that is available for a variety of mobile platforms but you will find an array of options by searching for "QR Reader" in your app store. Just keep in mind that if you use QR Codes in your class, your students may not know what to do with them. So it's important to explain the process and include a link to a QR Code reader in your syllabus or online course materials.

Here are a few examples of how QR Codes are being used in higher education:

SCVNGR Treks

Much like the gameful approach that inspired Dow Day, mobile devices are infusing some friendly competition into students' college orientations. Clarkson University is one of several colleges that has used an existing mobile app

Figure 6.7 QR code.

called SCAVNGR (http://www.scvngr.com) to create customized, scavenger-hunt like treks for students and their families upon their first visit to campus. This 21st-century student orientation experience is quite unique from the guided tours of yesterday but shares the same goals: to acquaint students with the campus, culture, and history. Clarkson has created several treks that students and their families can participate in and can earn prizes (gift certificates, free meals, coupons) by completing challenges that are bundled inside.

To "play" a student needs three things: 1) a smartphone, 2) the free SCVNGR app, and 3) a QR reader app. The college has also designed a way for users with feature phones (mobile phones without an internet connection) to play using text messaging.

The treks at Clarkson are planned to begin and end on specific dates, creating more of a community experience as prospective students and their families embark upon them at the same time. When a trek is begun, the student is given directions to a particular campus site. When they arrive at the location, they must complete one or more challenges, which could include taking a picture at the location and sharing it online, answering questions about the site, or scanning a QR Code on site. This process continues, completed challenges accumulate, and prizes are earned!

Field Experiments

Jason Farman, Assistant Professor of American Studies and Distinguished Faculty Fellow at the University of Maryland and author of *Mobile Interface Theory: Embodied Space and Locative Media*, blends the use of QR Codes and an app called 7Scenes (http://7scenes.com) to create what he calls "field experiments" designed to have his students interact with the campus using mobile media.

Farman's institution has followed in the footsteps of ACU by experimenting with one-to-one mobile programs. Most recently, Farman's program was selected for a one-to-one iPad pilot. In one experiment, as Farman explains, the students utilized their iPads to gain a "deeper sense of context for a space that they have become very familiar with."[13]

To get started with one of his field experiments, students need to locate and scan a QR Code attached to their professor's office door (serving to demonstrate that students know where his office is). The QR Code triggers the automatic download of the 7Scenes app onto the students' iPads. 7Scenes is an app that generates a location-based experience, allowing a user to attach content to maps that get pushed to other users to view and interact with when they are standing on that precise location.

As the students walked around their campus community, quiz questions, in the form of voice recordings from their professor, are pushed to their iPads. The questions provided information about the history behind historic buildings on campus that is usually left out of a students' college experience.

Geocaching

Another of Farman's field experiments involves taking his students on a geocaching adventure. The students use GPS coordinates and a tracking system on their mobile devices (or an app like Groundspeak: http://www.groundspeak.com) to locate tiny treasure stashes hidden around campus. The objective of this activity is, again, to demonstrate how interactions with digital space can transform one's relationship to and understanding of their material surroundings.

Geocaching expeditions can be activities integrated into just about any discipline. Imagine including a quiz question within a cache that a small team of students needs to find. By answering the quiz question, they could solve the missing coordinates for the next clue's location. For example, "The number of letters in the social media tool that Tweets." By solving problems and answering questions together, students learn to collaborate with a team, demonstrate their understanding of course concepts, and have fun at the same time.

But wait! Before you start building that high tech scavenger hunt, you'll want to visit http://www.geocaching.com/guide to learn the community groundrules for the sport. There are some important guidelines you'll want to be sure to model!

Virtually Enhanced Exhibitions

Abilene Christian University uses QR Codes in on-campus exhibits to link students to songs, videos, and websites, as well as searches within their library catalog.

Connecting Physical and Virtual Library Services

Lawrence University provides a support site for students to orient them to QR Codes (http://www.lawrence.edu/library/qr.shtml) and has them posted in various locations throughout the library to connect students with songs from their online music database, information about upcoming library events, and a virtual library tour.

Tablets: Peering Into the Future

As noted earlier, a tablet PC is a mobile device that is significantly larger than a smartphone, yet still easily portable and handheld. The dazzling, much larger, high definition screen on a tablet makes it an attractive and convenient option for media consumption (eBooks and videos) and their support of mobile apps allow a user to create a low-cost, highly customized suite of applications.

What's key to the integration of tablets into college learning is the realization and understanding that they *are not laptops*. If tablets are provided to students as part of their registration package, professors will need to understand that the devices will not replace laptops for note-taking. If a student's classroom experience is anchored in note-taking then a tablet is *not* the right device for that class. When the University of Notre Dame experimented with using iPads in a management class, students simply didn't use the device because typing on its shiny surface is time consuming.[14] That doesn't make iPads failures. It means they were not aligned with the students' objectives.

Tablets aren't good for lecture-based classes. Neither are smartphones. That's a fundamental theme of this entire book. The success of integrating mobile devices into college classrooms is contingent upon reinventing college learning. When classroom learning is intertwined with student-centered, collaborative, inquiry-driven activities, then we'll see some exciting innovations surface. Here's a peek at a few existing examples.

Pepperdine University

In 2010, Pepperdine University launched a study to evaluate the effectiveness of the iPad as a learning tool. The study included four professors who each taught two sections of the same course. The objective of the study was to assess the iPad's potential to impact social learning, engagement, and collaboration. Students in each of the classes were provided with an iPad that was preloaded with a suite of apps selected for that particular class.

The results of the study varied by class. The greatest success was seen in classes that were more likely to engage students in group work, were facilitated by an instructor who was open to the idea of changing the way the course was taught, and used apps that were effectively aligned with the functions required by the students (for example, students who were required to draw diagrams and were provided with an app that facilitated this activity).

The most notable difference was the increase in student-to-student interaction that was visible in the classroom. One student reflected, "You're more likely to help each other when it's portable and you can see what each other is doing." The results of the study also validate the importance of aligning a technology or tool with a clear purpose, ensuring that faculty understand how to use the technology (or students will be more frustrated and disengaged), and that students will engage in the use of technology in a learning environment when they are led by an instructor who can explain why it's being used and how to use it.

For an overview of the Pepperdine iPad Study, go to: http://community.pepper dine.edu/it/tools/ipad/research/default.htm.

Seton Hill University

Seton Hill University began providing iPads to all their full-time students (and faculty) in 2010. Their site http://www.ipadonthehill.com provides helpful samples of how the iPads are being used by students across disciplines. For example, art history students use the Art Authority app (http://www.artauthority.net, $9.99) in class to have access to thousands of art works. When a student pulls up a particular art work, the app responds with an array of additional samples made by the same artist, expanding a student's perspective and understanding of an artist's stylistic development over time and far exceeding the number of images printed in a textbook.

Music students use an app called Instruments (http://www.musicinreach.com/instruments.html, $2.99) to learn the fingering for a variety of instruments outside of class. The app presents digital sheet music to a user. By clicking on a note with your finger, the app presents a graphic representation of the proper fingering for a selected instrument. A digital keyboard app turns an iPad's glossy screen into a digital piano. Students can use the app to help them analyze music recordings and identify the notes and pitches as part of their homework. And while the musicians play, they can glance down at the Cleartune app (http://www.bitcount.com, $3.99) on their iPad to see if they're playing in tune.

English students might use the app Popplet (http://popplet.com, $4.99) to create visual mindmaps to brainstorm and organize ideas for essays and to analyze the plots of books. Simply use the app to create a bubble to represent a topic and then generate mini-bubbles to represent ideas or concepts to support each topic. Each bubble or mini-bubble included in one of the Popplet maps can be easily moved with a gesture of your hand, allowing the visual maps to be as fluid as writing with a pencil on paper.

Supporting *All* Learners

Up until now, students with cognitive disorders and physical disabilities have relied upon assistive technologies to improve access to and understanding of course materials. Arguably, assistive technologies exist because our learning environments have been *exclusive*—not designed to meet the unique needs of all learners. That *may* be shifting. Today, the multisensory experience and gesture-based commands that drive smartphones and tablets are presenting some exciting opportunities for supporting the needs of learners who are challenged by computers that are controlled by keyboards and mouses and have been used mostly to deliver text-dominated content.

There are an array of examples that demonstrate these possibilities. First, software that is operated by voice commands and applications that translate text-to-voice are included on all iPhones and iPads, turning these mobile devices into valuable resources to blind people. Specifically, Ariadne GPS (http://www.ariadnegps.eu/) is a talking map app that informs a walking user which streets or addresses are being passed and alerts him when he has reached his destination. HeyTell (http://heytell.com) is a free app that invites smartphone users to engage in voice-based, walkie-talkie-like conversation exchanges, providing voice alternative to text messaging that is not accessible to many communities of users. ColorID (http://www.greengar.com) uses a camera to analyze colors in one's surroundings, providing blind users information that reveals when an electronic device is fully charged, the color of the pants on the hanger, or the ripeness of a banana. And LookTel (http://www.looktel.com) is an app that verbally verifies the denomination of dollar bills, providing a way for a blind user to ensure she has received the correct change at the grocery store. Today, with the help of mobile apps, blind users are able to independently understand their environment in ways not possible before.

Further, the ability to navigate multi-sensory mobile apps with hand gestures is breaking new grounds for children with autism who do not possess the motor skills necessary to manipulate a mouse and keyboard.[15] While in the past children with autism who are unable to speak have lived in an isolated world, today they can use apps that can speak for them and, in the process, help them learn the foundations of verbal communication. Other apps are helping children with autism to learn to handle social situations and develop fine motor skills. For years, computers have provided similar features but it's the fact that a child can have a smartphone or tablet available anywhere at anytime and make something happen with a swipe of a finger that makes these apps so much more accessible to them.

Further, as video and voice become more integrated with daily communications, we will continue to see increased opportunities for students with cognitive learning disabilities. "Learning disabilities" is an umbrella term that describes an array of neurobiological disorders that affect the way the brain receives, processes, stores, expresses and responds to information. Personally, I prefer the term "learning differences," as these learning patterns have always been present in humans and it's merely our society's standardization of learning that fosters the perception that they are "disorders." Some common learning disabilities include dyslexia, dysgraphia, and dyscalculia, which, according to the Learning Disabilities Association of America (LDAA) affect about 10% of the US population.

Historically, formalized education has systematically filtered out students with non-traditional learning patterns—leaving them to feel like failures, unable to succeed or barely get by in school. This is especially true for students who go undiagnosed and don't have the chance to learn strategies to support their individualized needs. In fact, a student in the United States with a learning disability is three times more likely to drop out of high school.[16] According to the Dyslexia Research Institute, only about five in every one hundred dyslexics receive accommodations, a problem that is complicated by the fact that dyslexia often coincides with ADHD. Within our society, behavioral issues tied to ADHD are more likely to be diagnosed and treated, leaving the difficulty of reading and writing that dyslexia presents a silent challenge for students to deal with. As a result, many dyslexics can pass literacy tests in school but grow up to comprise the 44 million adults with the lowest levels of literacy in the United States.

The application of mobile apps into college-level learning supports Universal Design for Learning (UDL), which, as defined in the Higher Education Opportunity Act of 2008, is a "scientifically valid framework for guiding educational practice." [17] Designed to support brain research, the three principles of UDL stress the importance of developing learning environments that present information in multiple ways, offer students options in how they express their abilities, and incorporate variety in learning activities to promote engagement. The integration of mobile apps into college (and primary/secondary) learning provides promising strategies for developing learning environments that support the UDL framework.

As I write this, my online students are choosing between leaving voice, video, or text comments from their computer, telephone, or iPhone. Blending in multi-sensory learning activities breaks up the reading and writing that is such a big part of an online class. Reading and writing can pose significant challenges for students with learning differences. In those video comments, I *see* and *hear* my online students with dyslexia shine as they reflect through spoken language about our course topics. And the compelling ideas and insights they share in those videos contrast sharply with the struggled writing I read on their blogs and in their papers.

Imagine, just for a moment, if every year of your formalized educational experience taught you that *you were incapable of learning*. That's the reality of so many college students with learning disabilities. While students with learning disabilities may be present in any class, they are much more likely to attend public 2-year and 4-year institutions.[18] Despite their painful and demoralizing journey through school, I am consistently moved and inspired to see so many of my own challenged students with the passion and drive to pursue a college degree. And for that reason, I advocate on their behalf. *All* students deserve the opportunity to learn and pursue their dreams of a college degree. Mobile learning could play a central role in increasing the number of college educated people, as it provides avenues to more diversified, inclusive learning environments that support the needs of more students.

These reflections make me pause and loop back to the moment in 2009 when I sat listening to Bill Rankin present about ACU's initiative to give iPhones to their incoming freshmen. At that time, when I imagined using mobile devices in my classes or on my campus, I saw all kinds of red flags because I specifically targeted them as inaccessible tools that would leave students with learning differences or physical disabilities behind. While we do need to proceed with caution and we should never assume any application is accessible to everyone, I have to say that *I love the fact that I was wrong*. I love that the iPhone and iPad I use to take voice notes, play Scrabble with my friends, get directions, receive alerts about meetings and appointments, connect with my social networks, read the latest news, listen to my customized radio station, take and share pictures and videos, and interact with my students through voice and video are the same devices that are empowering cognitively challenged and disabled people of all ages.

Educators today have the power to change the world. The way we respond to the opportunities that emerging technologies hold will set the tone for the future of college learning. Can it get more exciting than that? :)

A Culture of Learning

Web 2.0 technologies, social media, and mobile devices have reinvented our learning options. Today, you don't need to enroll in a college or university to become a subject-matter expert on a particular topic. On the contrary, any person with access to the internet, regardless of age, race, ethnicity, or income level, is connected to more information in an instant than previous generations were exposed to in an entire lifetime. Colleges and universities will need to reinvent themselves to demonstrate their worth in this new culture of learning.

In the coming years, college classrooms will continue to transform. Textbooks will be challenged by open content, fueled by a new culture that values openness and sharing. Learning will continue to evolve from a process grounded in transferring information from subject-matter expert to novice followed by a quiz or test to an experience in which a student acquires new skills and demonstrates these proficiencies by creating new content that is commented on by one's peers and instructor. We will also see diversification in how learners validate their skills to prospective employers as college degrees are joined by digital badges.

And while our new culture of learning is exciting, thrilling, and inspiring, its ability to deliver quick answers, thought-provoking questions, and connect lifelong learners around the globe will challenge the cultural role that colleges and universities have played in our society for centuries. The 21st century will be an exciting journey in which *you* have an important role to play.

Chapter 7

Online Resources

Link to this book's online resources: http://www.teachingwithemergingtech.com.

From the online resources page, you have access to a continually evolving collection of tools, reviews, updates, showcases, videos, interviews, and trainings. The resources are compiled by the author from a variety of sources and are shared online, rather than in print, in an effort to ensure they are current. They are collected using some of the content curation tools featured in Chapter 5, which will give you an opportunity to see these tools in use, use them to curate your own collections from the shared resources, and post public comments. The site also includes instructions about how to use the tags to navigate the bookmarks and find the resources that meet your individual needs. For example, you can peruse the pages tagged with "bptet" to view all the bookmarks associated with the book, "ch5" to view only resources in support of Chapter 5, or view resources that relate to a broader term like "mobile." Remember, check back frequently to stay current.

Alternatively, you also have the option to follow me on Twitter @brocansky or you may search Twitter for the book's hashtag, #bptet. And, if you are a Twitter user, I invite you to share your own resources with us all by including the hashtag in your book-related Tweets. See you online!

Figure 7.1
Tag word cloud.
Created with
Wordle.net.

Notes

Preface

1 Smith, A. (2011). Smartphone adoption and usage. [survey]. Pew Internet & American Life Project. Retrieved from http://pewinternet.org/Reports/2011/Smartphones.aspx.

Introduction

1 Barr, R. B. & Tagg, J. (1995) "From Teaching to Learning—A New Paradigm for Undergraduate Education." *Change Magazine*, 27 (6): 12–25.
2 For more information about the history of the term "flipped classroom," see: http://blendedclassroom.blogspot.com/2011/05/history-of-flipped-class.html.
3 Rainie, L. (2011). "The State of Millennials," Pew Internet & American Life Project. Retrieved from: http://www.pewinternet.org/Presentations/2011/Jul/Millennials.aspx.
4 Pew Internet Research Center (Nov 23–Dec 21, 2010), Internet & American Life Project, Social side of the internet. Retrieved from: http://www.pewinternet.org/Reports/2011/The-Social-Side-of-the-Internet/Summary.aspx.
5 Center for Generational Studies FAQ. Retrieved from: http://www.generational diversity.com/faq.html.
6 Project Tomorrow. (2011) "Speak Up 2010: National Findings, K-12 Students and Parents." Retrieved from: http://www.tomorrow.org/speakup/.
7 YouTube press statistics. Retrieved from: http://www.youtube.com/t/press_statistics.
8 Hirshberg (2009, Dec 11) Howard Rheingold on technology and education. [video file]. Retrieved from: http://youtube/bI6Q_1V7XJ8.
9 To download the list of references for this particular "Brain Rule," visit: http://www.brain rules.net/pdf/references_multisensory.pdf.
10 To download list of references for this particular "Brain Rule," visit: http://www.brain rules.net/pdf/references_vision.pdf.

Chapter 1

1 Smith, S. & Borreson Caruso, J. Introduction by Kim, J. (2010). The ECAR Study of Undergraduate Students and Information Technology, 2010. (Research Study). Boulder, CO: EDUCAUSE Center for Applied Research. Retrieved from: http://www.educause.edu/ecar.
2 Davidson, C., Goldberg, D. T., Jones, Z. M. (2009). *The Future of Thinking: Learning Institutions in a Digital Age*. From the John D. and Catherine T. MacArthur Foundation Reports on Digital Media and Learning. MIT Press: Cambridge, MA.
3 Wesch, M. [mwesch]. (2011, Jan 26). The Visions of Students Today. [video remix]. Retrieved from http://www.youtube.com/user/mwesch#p/u/0/-_XNG3Mndww.

4 Wolfram Alpha [website]. Accessed on February 20, 2012 from: http://www.wolframalpha.com/entities/web_domains/ratemyprofessors.com/98/2v/kh/.

5 Brigham Young University's "Copyright 101" offers an exceptionally concise and useful online module about copyright that includes self-assessments: http://lib.byu.edu/departs/copyright/tutorial/intro/page1.htm.

6 The Constitution of the United States of America. Retrieved from: http://caselaw.lp.findlaw.com/data/constitution/articles.html.

7 Cornell has shared a helpful online table to assist with identifying when a work enters public domain: http://copyright.cornell.edu/resources/publicdomain.cfm.

8 Center for Social Media. (n.d.) Remix Culture: Fair Use is Your Friend. [video recording]. Retrieved from: http://www.centerforsocialmedia.org/fair-use/videos/podcasts/remix-culture-fair-use-your-friend.

9 For a lighthearted portrayal of the trials and tribulations of a documentary filmmaker navigating traditional copyright regulations, see Duke's Center for the Study of the Public Domain, "Tales From the Public Domain: BOUND BY LAW?" http://www.law.duke.edu/cspd/comics/.

10 Creative Commons CC Affiliate Network wiki. Accessed on August 23, 2011 from: http://wiki.creativecommons.org/CC_Affiliate_Network.

11 Creative Commons. (n.d.). History. Retrieved from: https://creativecommons.org/about/history.

12 Creative Commons. (n.d.). License chooser. Retrieved from: http://creativecommons.org/choose/.

Chapter 2

1 Hargadon, S. (2011, June). Open Learning: The Future of Education. [Keynote presentation]. Online Teaching Conference, Orange Coast College.

2 Samson, P. J. (2010, April-June). "Deliberate Engagement of Laptops in Large Lecture Classes to Improve Attentiveness and Engagement." *Computers in Education* (1) 2.

3 Ibid.

4 Ibid.

5 For a succinct checklist to assist with evaluating web-based content for 508 compliance, visit: http://www.epa.gov/inter508/toolkit/508_compliance_toolkit_web_apps.htm – checklist.

6 University of Washington, Web Accessibility. http://www.washington.edu/accessibility/web.html.

7 Brown, C. & Keegan, S. The Three C's of Accessibility and Distance Education, High Tech Training Center. [report]. Retrieved from http://www.htctu.net/publications/articles/three_cs_111804.pdf.

8 Ibid.

9 Slideshare. Terms of Services. Accessed on Sept 22, 2011 from: http://www.slideshare.net/terms.

10 View the TrustE program requirements here: http://www.truste.com/privacy-program-requirements/index.html.

11 Ning. Applications Terms of Use. Accessed on Sept 26, 2011 from: http://www.ning.com/about/legal/thirdpartyapptos/.

12 YouTube. Privacy Notice. Accessed on Sept 26, 2011 from: http://www.youtube.com/static?hl=en&template=privacy.

13 Jones, J. B. (2011, July 28). Use Collusion to Learn About Web Privacy, ProfHacker. [blog post]. http://chronicle.com/blogs/profhacker/use-collusion-to-learn-about-web-privacy/34977.

Chapter 5

1 Sullivan, D. (2011, Sept 8). Twitter CEO, Dick Costolo's "State of the Union" address. Search Engine Land. [blog post]. Retrieved from: http://searchengineland.com/live-blog-twitter-ceo-dick-costolos-informal-business-address-92207.

2 Atkinson, C. (2009). How People are Using Twitter and Social Media and Changing Presentations Forever. Berkeley, CA: New Riders Press.

3 Bruff, D. (2011, May 17). Backchannel (and me) in the New York Times. Agile Learning. [blog post]. Retrieved from: http://derekbruff.org/?p=979.

4 Davidson, C. & Goldbert, D. T. (2010). *The Future of Thinking: Learning Institutions in a Digital Age*. The MIT Press. Cambridge, MA.

5 Doyle, C. (n.d.) Twitter as an enabler of critical thinking. Vanderbilt University Center for Teaching. [blog post]. Retrieved from: http://cft.vanderbilt.edu/2011/10/twitter-as-an-enabler-of-critical-thinking/.

6 To view a VoiceThread I created to showcase examples of how I've used VoiceThread in my classes, excerpts of student contributions, student feedback about VoiceThread, and survey results about VoiceThread, go to: http://voicethread.com/share/908650/.

7 Ettzevoglou, N. & McBride, J. (2009). "Ning and Writing to Learn." *Educause Quarterly* 32(4). Retrieved from: http://www.educause.edu/EDUCAUSE+Quarterly/EDUCAUSE QuarterlyMagazineVolum/NingandWritingtoLearn/192956.

8 Ibid.

9 Ibid.

10 Ibid.

11 Ibid.

12 To read Bruff's recap of the faculty workshop referred to here, go to: http://chronicle. com/blogs/profhacker/revolution-or-evolution-social-technologies-and-change-in-higher-education/29304.

13 Bruff, D. (2012, Jan 8). Social Bookmarking 101. Math 216: Statistics for Engineering. [blog post]. Retrieved from: http://derekbruff.org/blogs/math216/?p=52.

Chapter 6

1 Johnson, L., Adams, S., and Cummins, M. (2012). The NMC Horizon Report: 2012 Higher Education Edition. Austin, Texas: The New Media Consortium. Retrieved from: http:// www.nmc.org.

2 Abilene Christian University, ACU Connected website. Retrieved from: http:// www.acu.edu/technology/mobilelearning.

3 Abilene Christian University website. Retrieved from: http://www.acu.edu/technology/ mobilelearning/vision/.

4 Smith, Aaron. (2012). Nearly half of American adults are smartphone owners. Pew Internet & American Life Project. Retrieved from: http://pewinternet.org/Reports/2012/ Smartphone-Update-2012.aspx

5 Ericsson Press Release (2010, Jul 9). "Mobile Subscriptions Hit 5 Billion Mark." Retrieved from: http://www.ericsson.com/jm/news/1430616.

6 Cited as a "Key Trend" in the 2011 Horizon Report by the New Media Consortium. Retrieved from: http://wp.nmc.org/horizon2011/sections/trends/.

7 Wentworth, D. & Green, M. (2011, July). "Mobile Learning: Anyplace, Anytime." T + D. p. 25.

8 Parry, D. (2011, March/April). "Mobile Perspectives: On Teaching Mobile Literacy." *EDUCAUSE Review*, 46(2).

9 Retrieved from: http://148apps.biz/app-store-metrics/?mpage=appcount.

10 Schaffhauser, D. (2010, October 5). "Purdue Students Hook Into Facebook for Study Groups." Campus Technology. Retrieved from: http://campustechnology.com/articles/ 2010/10/05/purdue-students-hook-into-facebook-for-study-groups.aspx.

11 Medina, J. (2008). *Brain Rules*. Seattle, WA: Pear Press.
12 Retrieved from: http://blogs.edweek.org/edweek/schooled_in_sports/2012/01/strong_evidence_of_link_between_physical_activity_academic_success.html.
13 Farman, J. (2012, Feb 9) Encouraging distraction? Classroom experiments with mobile media. Guest post on the ProfHacker blog. Retrieved from: http://chronicle.com/blogs/profhacker/encouraging-distraction-classroom-experiments-with-mobile-media/38454.
14 Wieder, B. (2011, March 13). "iPads Could Hinder Teaching, Professors Say." *Chronicle of Higher Education*. Technology blog. Retrieved from: http://chronicle.com/article/iPads-for-College-Classrooms-/126681/.
15 Melendez, L. (2011). "Autism Community Sees Promise in iPad Apps." ABC 7 News website. Retrieved from: http://abclocal.go.com/kgo/story?section=news/education&id=8374840.
16 Office of Special Education and Rehabilitative Services, 23rd Annual Report to Congress: http://www2.ed.gov/about/reports/annual/osep/2001/index.html.
17 National Center on Universal Design for Learning. (2011, April 14). How has UDL been defined? Retrieved from: http://www.udlcenter.org/aboutudl/udldefined.
18 Raue, K. & Lewis, L. (2011, June). Report. Students with disabilities at degree-granting postsecondary institutions. National Center for Education Statistics, Institute of Education Sciences. US Department of Education.

Index